Windows 8: Out of the Box

Mike Halsey

Beijing · Cambridge · Farnham · Köln · Sebastopol · Tokyo

Windows 8: Out of the Box
by Mike Halsey

Copyright © 2012 Mike Halsey. All rights reserved.
Printed in the United States of America.

Published by O'Reilly Media, Inc., 1005 Gravenstein Highway North, Sebastopol, CA 95472.

O'Reilly books may be purchased for educational, business, or sales promotional use. Online editions are also available for most titles (*http://my.safaribookson line.com*). For more information, contact our corporate/institutional sales department: 800-998-9938 or *corporate@oreilly.com*.

Editor: Rachel Roumeliotis	**Cover Designer:** Karen Montgomery
Production Editor: Rachel Steely	**Interior Designer:** David Futato
Copyeditor: Jessica Jonas	**Illustrators:** Robert Romano and Rebecca Demarest
Technical Editor: Sander Berkouwer	
Proofreader: Rachel Steely	

October 2012:   First Edition.

Revision History for the First Edition:
    2012-09-27   First release

See *http://oreilly.com/catalog/errata.csp?isbn=9781449326647* for release details.

ISBN: 978-1-449-32664-7

[LSI]

1348775959

For Darren, Victoria, and Baby
Gilbert. Happy days.

—Mike Halsey

Table of Contents

Preface

Audience

This book is for anybody who is coming to use Windows 8 for the first time, perhaps through purchasing a new computer or a first tablet, and who wants to know how to get the very best user experience from this new version of Windows.

Assumptions This Book Makes

This book assumes that you have a little prior computing experience and that you understand the basics, such as how to use a mouse and keyboard. You should not need any more experience than this. It is probable that in the past, you have used a computer only for light tasks such as email and surfing the web.

Contents of This Book

This book will guide you through using Windows 8 by focusing on the things you will most likely want to do with your Windows 8 computer. These include getting on the Internet, using email and web pages safety, importing and editing digital photographs from your camera, and making sure your children are protected when they're online.

Conventions Used in This Book

The following typographical conventions are used in this book:

Italic
> Indicates new terms, URLs, email addresses, filenames, and file extensions.

`Constant width`

> Used for program listings, as well as within paragraphs to refer to program elements such as variable or function names, databases, data types, environment variables, statements, and keywords.

`Constant width bold`

> Shows commands or other text that should be typed literally by the user.

`Constant width italic`

> Shows text that should be replaced with user-supplied values or by values determined by context.

 This icon signifies a tip, suggestion, or general note.

 This icon indicates a warning or caution.

Using Code Examples

This book is here to help you get your job done. In general, you may use the code in this book in your programs and documentation. You do not need to contact us for permission unless you're reproducing a significant portion of the code. For example, writing a program that uses several chunks of code from this book does not require permission. Selling or distributing a CD-ROM of examples from O'Reilly books does require permission. Answering a question by citing this book and quoting example code does not require permission. Incorporating a significant amount of example code from this book into your product's documentation does require permission.

We appreciate, but do not require, attribution. An attribution usually includes the title, author, publisher, and ISBN. For example: "*Windows 8: Out of the Box* by Mike Halsey (O'Reilly). Copyright 2012 Mike Halsey, 978-1-449-32664-7."

If you feel your use of code examples falls outside fair use or the permission given above, feel free to contact us at *permissions@oreilly.com*.

Safari® Books Online

Safari Safari Books Online (*www.safaribooksonline.com*) is an on-demand digital library that delivers expert content in both book and video form from the world's leading authors in technology and business.

Technology professionals, software developers, web designers, and business and creative professionals use Safari Books Online as their primary resource for research, problem solving, learning, and certification training.

Safari Books Online offers a range of product mixes and pricing programs for organizations, government agencies, and individuals. Subscribers have access to thousands of books, training videos, and prepublication manuscripts in one fully searchable database from publishers like O'Reilly Media, Prentice Hall Professional, Addison-Wesley Professional, Microsoft Press, Sams, Que, Peachpit Press, Focal Press, Cisco Press, John Wiley & Sons, Syngress, Morgan Kaufmann, IBM Redbooks, Packt, Adobe Press, FT Press, Apress, Manning, New Riders, McGraw-Hill, Jones & Bartlett, Course Technology, and dozens more. For more information about Safari Books Online, please visit us online.

How to Contact Us

Please address comments and questions concerning this book to the publisher:

O'Reilly Media, Inc.
1005 Gravenstein Highway North
Sebastopol, CA 95472
800-998-9938 (in the United States or Canada)
707-829-0515 (international or local)
707-829-0104 (fax)

We have a web page for this book, where we list errata, examples, and any additional information. You can access this page at *http://oreil.ly/Windows_8 _OutofBox*.

To comment or ask technical questions about this book, send email to *bookquestions@oreilly.com*.

For more information about our books, courses, conferences, and news, see our website at *http://www.oreilly.com*.

Find us on Facebook: *http://facebook.com/oreilly*

Follow us on Twitter: *http://twitter.com/oreillymedia*

Watch us on YouTube: *http://www.youtube.com/oreillymedia*

How to Contact the Author

Mike has an open mailbag and always welcomes questions and comments from readers. He sincerely hopes you have enjoyed this book and that you will consider reviewing it online.

Please visit Mike's website at: *http://www.thelongclimb.com*.

Find Mike on Facebook: *www.facebook.com/HalseyMike*

Follow Mike on Twitter: *www.twitter.com/HalseyMike*

Watch Mike's videos on YouTube: *www.youtube.com/TheLongClimb*

Watch Mike's webcasts: *http://www.oreilly.com/webcasts*

Acknowledgments

With thanks to Sander Berkouwer for your valuable contribution.

CHAPTER 1

Using Windows 8

Windows 8 is very different to previous versions of Windows from Microsoft primarily in that it has a new look that's been redesigned to be easy to use with touch as well as with a mouse and keyboard. For the first time, it's no longer necessary to understand how small and fiddly drop-down menus work, or to understand how to control programs using complicated desktop menus where you have to manage and juggle multiple programs on your screen at one time.

Windows 8 can be operated by a keyboard and mouse, but it is best used with a touchscreen computer or tablet, and it is here that you will benefit from the richest experience.

Everything has changed to make it not just easier to find and control documents, apps, and programs, but to make overall control of Windows and your settings simpler. At last, you don't need to be a technical user to get the best out of using Windows.

When you use Windows 8 on your computer, laptop, or tablet for the first time, you'll notice how different it looks and works. This new look makes it easier for you to see what's going on in your online life at a glance: Live Tiles can show you information about your email, calendar, instant messaging, social networking, sports, news, and much more, all without ever leaving the new Start screen.

In this chapter, I'll demonstrate what these new interface elements are and how to use them.

Top Tips from This Chapter

1. You can open menus and options on the Start screen by swiping with your finger from any edge of the screen.
2. Move your mouse to the corners of the screen to display options and menus.
3. On your keyboard, you can hold down the *Windows Key* in the bottom left of the keyboard and press *Z* or *C* to open menus and options.

The Start Screen Versus the Desktop: What You Need to Know

I've already mentioned the new interface in Windows 8, the Start screen. The *traditional* Windows desktop still exists, though, so that you can use software you're used to in Windows 7.

There is a new style of program in Windows 8, however, called an App. These apps (or applications) run full screen and are easier and friendlier to use than desktop programs. Windows 8 comes preinstalled with many apps for email, calendar, news, and so on, and you can download more from the new Windows Store. You will see the *Store* tile on the Start screen. I will show you how to use the Windows Store and install apps and programs in Chapter 4.

If you are using a Windows 8 tablet, you will only be able to install apps from the Windows store. You can't install desktop software on tablet computers. The only exception to this is Windows 8 Pro tablets; you should check the documentation that came with your tablet to see which type of device you have.

Starting Windows 8

When Windows 8 starts, you will see the lock screen (Figure 1-1). This displays the time and date, and can also show extra information, including how many emails you have and what your next calendar appointment is.

 You open the lock screen by swiping upwards on the screen with your finger if you have a touch display, or by pressing any key on the computer's keyboard.

Figure 1-1. The Windows 8 lock screen

When you first started using your computer, you may have set a password for your user account. If you did, you will be asked for this before you can unlock the computer. You can also create a numerical password for Windows 8 or use a picture password. I will show you how to do this in Chapter 12.

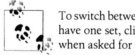 To switch between a standard password, PIN, or picture if you have one set, click/touch *sign-in-options* at the sign-in screen when asked for your password.

Finding Your Way Around the New Start Screen

The Start screen (Figure 1-2) in Windows 8 is based around square and rectangular-colored blocks called Tiles. When clicked or tapped, each one starts an app. The app will then perform a specific task such as sending and receiving email, viewing web pages, editing photographs, or playing a game. The Start screen pans left to right across your screen.

Figure 1-2. The Windows 8 Start screen

 Swipe left and right with your finger to pan across the Start screen. If you are using a mouse, you will see a scroll bar at the bottom of the screen when you move the mouse. Click/Touch and drag this left and right to look around the Start screen. You can also use the scroll wheel (up and down) on your mouse to move left and right on the Start screen.

As you look around the Start screen, you will see that some Tiles change occasionally to display text or images. These are Live Tiles, which give you information from inside the app or show you what is new or changed, such as giving you a message.

These messages can include details of new emails or social network messages, informing you of the number of updates that are available for your apps in the Windows Store or giving you news headlines.

You can rearrange Tiles on the Start screen by dragging them around and dropping them into a new location, which can help you organize them to best suit you. I will show you how to organize the Start screen in Chapter 4.

When you drag a Tile between groups, you will see a colored vertical bar appear. If you drop the Tile onto this bar, you can create a new group. This can be useful to separate apps. For example, you can separate games, websites, and so on.

Using the Charms Menu

The Start Button from previous versions of Windows (sometimes known as the Windows Orb), was previously located in the bottom left hand corner of your desktop screen, and had the function of finding and running programs. In Windows 8, it has moved to a new Charms menu (Figure 1-3). This pops out from the right side of the screen and contains icons for useful tasks in Windows 8.

You can open the Charms Menu by swiping in from the right of the screen with your finger or pressing *WindowsKey+C* on your keyboard (the WindowsKey is the key at the bottom left of your keyboard with the Windows logo on it). To open the Charms Menu with a mouse, move your mouse to the bottom right or the top right corner of the screen.

On the Charms Menu, you will find the following options:

- **Search** opens the search panel so you can find apps, documents, and Windows 8 Settings.
- **Share** allows you to share text, pictures, and more between Windows 8 apps.
- **Start** returns you to the Start screen; this is also available by pressing the Windows Key on your keyboard or the Windows button on your tablet computer.
- **Devices** allows you to work with printers, display projectors, and other hardware devices.
- **Settings** displays basic Windows 8 Settings and controls.

 You can also search for apps, settings, and files by typing directly at the Start screen. You do not need to open the Search panel.

Figure 1-3. The Charms menu

Using the App Bar

If you have used an earlier version of Windows, you might know that pressing the *right* mouse button can bring up a menu of options associated with an icon or program. In Windows 8 apps and on the Start screen, this *right-click* now displays the App Bar.

The App Bar (Figure 1-4), which is also available by swiping up from the bottom of your screen with your finger or swiping down from the top, contains menu options that are available for that app.

To open the App Bar with your mouse, right-click in an app or on the Start screen. To open the App Bar from your keyboard, press the *WindowsKey+Z*.

These options are the equivalent to drop-down menus in Windows desktop programs and can perform many functions, each of which depends on the context of where you are and what you are doing.

Figure 1-4. The App Bar in Windows 8

 To perform an action on a Tile on the Start screen, such as hiding it from the Start screen completely (I will show you how to organize apps and tiles on the Start screen in Chapter 4), you can right-click/touch on the Tile with your mouse, or touch and swipe downwards with your finger, and the App Bar will appear with options for actions you can perform on that Tile. You can open the App Bar from your keyboard by pressing *WindowsKey+Z* in any app or from the Start screen.

If ever you want to open a menu in an app or on the Start screen, you will do this from the App Bar. This is where all the controls for apps can be found.

Finding All the Apps in Windows 8

Not all the apps and software in Windows 8 will appear on the Start screen. For example, you may have chosen to hide a Tile to keep your Start screen tidy, or perhaps you don't use it regularly.

You can see all the apps that are installed in Windows 8, including Windows desktop programs, by *right-clicking* in any blank space on the Start screen (also by touching a blank space and dragging down) and then clicking *All Apps* on the app bar.

In the All Apps view (Figure 1-5), you will see every app and all your desktop software that is installed on the computer. The apps that appear on the left of the screen and your desktop software on the right, are organized into clearly labelled categories to make things easy to find. You can move left and right in the All Apps view as you would on the Start screen.

 If you want to pin an app or program back on the Start screen, *right-click* (touch and drag down) on it and select *Pin to Start* from the App Bar

Figure 1-5. Finding all apps in Windows 8

Switching Between Running Apps in Windows 8

You can press the Windows Key on your keyboard or the Start icon in the Charms menu at any time to return to the Start screen, but you can also switch between apps by dragging the previous app in from the left of the screen with your finger. With a keyboard, you can use the *WindowsKey+Tab* keys to switch between running apps.

Docking Apps to the Left or Right of the Screen

When you drag an app in from the left of the screen with your finger, you will see a vertical bar appear in the left quarter or right quarter of the screen, depending on where you are dragging it at that point. Dropping an app when you see this bar will *dock* it to the far left or the far right of the screen (Figure 1-6).

Figure 1-6. Arranging apps on screen in Windows 8

If you then return to the Start screen by pressing the Windows Key, the next app you run will fill the remaining space, so you have two apps side by side. You can drag the vertical bar separating them left and right to switch the focus from one app to the other, or to move one app off the screen completely.

To dock apps side by side using a mouse (this also works with touch), drag the app from the top center of the screen toward the center of the screen. You will see the app change to a thumbnail image. You can now drag this thumbnail to the left or right of the screen and drop it when you see the vertical *dock* bar appear.

Logging Out Of and Locking Windows 8

If several people use Windows 8 on your computer and you want to switch to a different user, you can do this by clicking or touching your user icon and name in the top right of the Start screen. This will bring up a menu with three options (Figure 1-7).

Figure 1-7. The User Menu in Windows 8

 If you want to change your password, you can do this from the *Users* page in *PC Settings*. Click/Touch *Settings* in the Charms menu and then click *Change PC Settings* to access the options.

- **Change Account Picture** will allow you to choose a new picture for your account from images that you have on your computer.
- **Lock** will lock the computer so that a password, PIN, or picture password is needed to sign in again. This is useful if you are leaving your computer unattended for a while.
- **Sign-Out** will sign out of your account so that others can use the computer.

If you have multiple user accounts set up in Windows, perhaps for different members of your family (I will show you how to set these up in Chapter 10), these people will also appear in the user list when you click/touch your name in the top right of the Start screen. You can switch directly to another user by clicking their icon (you will *not* be logged out). This means that if you have any files or documents open that you have not saved, they might be lost if another user then shuts the computer down. They will be warned, however, by Windows 8 if another user is still logged in when they turn the computer off.

Using Touch Gestures in Windows 8

I have already shown you some of the touch gestures you can use in Windows 8, including touching a Tile to open it and touching and dragging down to select it.

There are other gestures you can use, including two finger pinch actions to zoom in and out (pinch in to zoom out and pinch out to zoom in).

To select an item and open App Bar options for it on the Start screen, touch it and drag it downward slightly. This is slightly different if you are using touch in desktop programs where you should touch and hold the item; this will simulate a mouse right-click.

Using Windows 8 with a Keyboard and Mouse

If you are using Windows 8 with a keyboard and mouse, there are several time-saving shortcuts that you can use instead of touch gestures.

- *Right mouse click* or press the *WindowsKey+Z* to display the App Bar in apps and at the Start screen
- Press the *WindowsKey+C* to open the Charms Menu
- Press the *WindowsKey+Tab* to switch between running apps

You can also move your mouse to the four corners of the screen; these are called hot corners, and each one will display different options. The top and bottom right-side corners will open the App Bar, and the top and bottom left corners will allow you to switch between running apps and opening the Start screen.

Using the On-Screen Keyboard

When you are using Windows 8 on a touchscreen, the on-screen keyboard will appear whenever you tap in a place where you would enter text, such as the address bar in Internet Explorer or a form on a website. When it appears, you will see the keyboard fill the full width of your screen, but if you're using your thumbs to type while holding your tablet in both hands, reaching the keys in the center of the keyboard can be tricky.

You can make using the on-screen keyboard easier to use when you are holding your tablet in both hands by clicking the keyboard icon in the bottom right of the on-screen keyboard (Figure 1-8) to display different layout options, including:

* The standard full screen width keyboard
* A thumbs keyboard where the keys are moved to the far left and right of the screen
* Handwriting recognition if your tablet comes with a stylus
* Hiding the on-screen keyboard

Figure 1-8. The Windows 8 on-screen keyboard

 You can select international characters on the on-screen keyboard by touching and holding a letter for one second. This will display accented letters that you can then touch to select.

Shutting Down and Restarting Windows 8

To restart or shut down Windows 8, follow these instructions.

* Open the Charms Menu
* Click/touch *Settings*

- In the panel that appears, click/touch *Power*
- In the menu that appears, click/touch *Shut Down*, *Restart*, or *Sleep* (Figure 1-9)

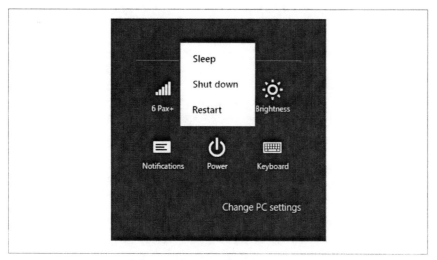

Figure 1-9. Restarting and shutting down Windows 8

Sleep puts your computer into a low-power *standby* state. This makes it very quick to switch on again, but it does consume a small amount of power, which can drain the battery on a laptop or tablet computer.

Summary

Windows 8 certainly offers a very new way of working, but it is simple and intuitive to use. In this chapter, I have shown you how to navigate the interface, launch apps, display menus, and move items to rearrange them, including arranging apps on your screen.

In Chapter 2, we will look at the things you will actually be doing with your computer, and I will show you how to connect to the Internet and check your email.

Using Email and the Internet

Whether you use a tablet, laptop, or desktop computer, you'll have it connected to the Internet. The Internet is now at the center of everything we do with our computers, from sending and receiving email to chatting and sharing photos and stories with friends and family. In Chapter 1, I showed you how to use the new interface in Windows 8. Now, let's see how you can get online and use the Internet Explorer web browser app and Windows 8's email app.

When you get a new computer, one of the very first things many people do is connect to the Internet to check email and catch up with friends and family. Windows 8 makes it very simple to get online, and all the tools you need are literally right at your fingertips.

Top Tips from This Chapter

1. If you sign into Windows 8 using the same login you use for your Hotmail or Live mail (this is called a Microsoft Account), many options in Windows 8 such as email, calendar, and the new Windows App Store will be automatically set up for you.
2. You can swipe left and right with your finger to automatically load the next and previous pages on a website.
3. The desktop version of Internet Explorer supports more features and allows you to organize many more Internet Favorites.

Getting Online with Windows 8

In your home, you will have an Internet router. This is the box that plugs into your phone line and provides Internet access for you. Some computers that remain static in the home, such as desktop PCs, can connect to these via a network cable. This is a physical cable connecting the computer to the router.

This is usually the best way to get a stable and super-quick Internet connection. If you use WiFi to connect to your computer, place your router in a location where you will get a good signal throughout the building and try to avoid putting it in a place where solid walls might block the signal.

Fixing WiFi Signal Problems

If you have a problem with your WiFi signal in your home, see if you can move your router to a better location, perhaps by using a telephone extension cable, or see if it is possible to install a *network cable* (that's all you need to ask for when purchasing one) that runs to the dead spots. Please note, though, that a cable does tie a computer to one location, some small laptops and tablets won't have a socket to plug the cable into, and trailing cables can also be a trip hazard.

If you connect a computer to your Internet router via a network cable, within a few seconds, you will have Internet access. If you don't, then try turning the router and PC off and on again.

Step by Step: Connecting to a Wireless Network

You will commonly want to connect your computer to the Internet via WiFi. You can also connect via a 3G or 4G connection if your laptop or tablet supports it, and if you have either a SIM card installed in your computer, or a wireless broadband USB stick plugged in (Figure 2-1).

1. Open the Charms Menu by swiping in from the right of your screen with your finger or pressing *WindowsKey+C* on your keyboard.

2. Click/Touch the *Settings* icon.

3. Click/Touch the *Network* icon, which is the first of six icons that will appear near the bottom right corner of your screen. It will say *Available* if Wireless Networks have been detected.

4. You will see Mobile Broadband (if your computer supports this) and WiFi networks listed separately. Click/Touch the name of the network you wish to connect to.

5. You may be asked for a password; enter it here.

 You can *right-click* (touch and hold) on any network in the available networks list to *Show [your] estimated data use*. This can be a useful way to ensure you don't go over your monthly data allowance on a 3G or 4G network.

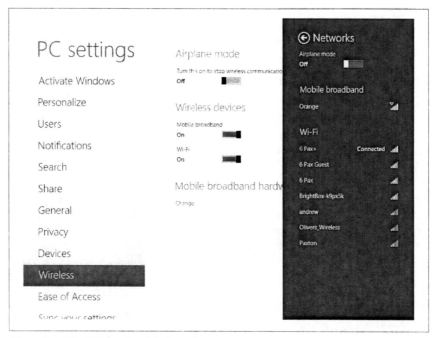

Figure 2-1. The WiFi and mobile broadband connection

When you connect to a network, you may be asked what type of network you are connecting to:

- **Home** networks should only be chosen when you are on your own WiFi network in your own home. This allows file sharing of files, documents, and printers between computers.

- **Work** networks allow certain sharing of files, documents, and printers, but they keep your own personal files safe from prying eyes.

- **Public** networks should always be selected if you are using WiFi in a coffee shop, on a train, or in another public location. This settings keeps your files, documents, and access to your computer safe and secure.

Additionally, any network where you do not need a password to get online is certainly insecure in that anybody can gain access to it. You should not allow the sharing of files on public networks or networks that are not protected by a password.

If your WiFi connection isn't working, try restarting your router and perhaps your computer as well. If you connect to the Internet via a WiFi or Mobile broadband USB dongle, try unplugging it from the computer and plugging it into a *different* USB port. Also, do you have Airplane Mode switched on? You can check this at the top right of the screen when connecting to a network.

Getting Quick Access to Your Email

Windows 8 comes with a new email app called Mail, which you will see on the Start screen. Here you can easily send and receive emails using either a keyboard and mouse or the on-screen keyboard. If you log into your computer using the same Microsoft Account you use to access your Hotmail or Live Mail account, then opening the *Mail* app on the Start screen will automatically display your email.

If you use a different email provider, perhaps Gmail, you can add your email to the Mail app by following these instructions:

1. Open the *People* app from the Start screen; it is in this app that you manage all your accounts for email, social networking, and messaging.

2. On the left of the screen, you will see a panel that allows you to connect new accounts to Windows 8 (Figure 2-2).

You can also manage your email accounts by opening the Charms menu in the Mail app and clicking/tapping the *Settings* icon. An *Accounts* link will then appear in the top right of the screen.

Using the Internet Explorer 10 App

Windows 8 comes with a copy of the Internet Explorer web browser. Internet Explorer is very simple to use (Figure 2-3). The address bar, where you type the addresses of the websites you want to visit, is at the bottom of the screen along with controls for *Back* (to the left of the address bar) to take you back a page and *Refresh* (to the right of the address bar) to reload the page. You can display these at any time by opening the App Bar.

Internet Explorer allows you to open multiple websites and switch between them using tabs. You can manage your tabs in Internet Explorer by opening

Figure 2-2. Connecting a new email account in Mail

the app bar and you will see thumbnail images of your open tabs at the top of the screen.

You can also use touch gestures in Internet Explorer to move backwards to previously loaded pages (*swipe left to right*) or to automatically move pages back and forth on a website (*swipe right to left*). This enables you to move through the pages of a website without needing to know what the next link is to click.

If you want to zoom into a part of a web page, or perhaps you are finding some text difficult to read or links too small to click or touch, the zoom feature can help here as well. You can make a two-finger pinch zoom gesture on the screen to zoom in and out of any part of a web page in both the app and desktop versions of Internet Explorer. If you use a keyboard and mouse, you will need to use the desktop version of Internet Explorer to employ the zoom, and the zoom controls can be found in the bottom right corner of the window.

To open a new browser tab in Internet Explorer, click/touch or tap the + button in the top right of the screen when the App Bar is open and the tabs are showing.

Figure 2-3. Internet Explorer 10 in Windows 8

 You can clean up all of your tabs by pressing the icon below the new tab button and selecting *Clean up Tabs* from the options that appear. This will automatically close all but the currently open tab.

When you click/touch the address bar, Internet Explorer will show you the websites you have visited recently and also any Favorites that you have saved. These favorites are automatically displayed on the Start screen.

These saved favorites appear both next to the list of recently visited websites, and also on the Start screen (Figure 2-4). You can organize and arrange these into groups, and I will show you how to do this in more detail in Chapter 4.

 You can open the app bar with your mouse in Internet Explorer by *right-clicking* in any blank space on a web page.

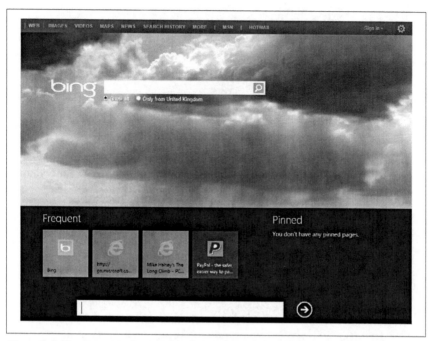

Figure 2-4. Viewing recently visited and pinned websites in IE10

Saving Your Favorite Websites to the Start Screen

To save a favorite website to the Start screen, open the App Bar in Internet Explorer and click/touch the *Pin* icon in the bottom right of the screen. A pop-up panel will display details of the current website and will ask you to confirm that you want to save (pin) it to the Start screen. You can later unpin websites the same way you remove apps, and I will show you how to do this in Chapter 4.

Internet Explorer and Plug-Ins

A plug-in is a small program or toolbar that you can add to your web browser to expand its functionality. The app version of Internet Explorer does not support browser plug-ins and toolbars such as Adobe Acrobat Reader, but the Flash player, which is commonly used for playing video and games, is already built into the browser.

Internet Explorer tells you if a website is known to be safe or unsafe by turning the address bar green or red. For shopping and banking websites, it will also display a padlock on the address bar if the website has adequate security. You should always look for a green address bar and/or the padlock when shopping or banking online.

Using InPrivate Mode

When you clean up your browser tabs in Internet Explorer, you will see a link to use InPrivate Mode. This is a special secure mode of Internet Explorer that prevents the browser from tracking where you have been, and also stops the website placing any tracking files, known as cookies, on your computer.

InPrivate Mode is especially useful for birthdays and holidays when you're shopping for presents and surprises, and you don't want other people who use your computer to know what you're getting them.

Internet Explorer on the Desktop

Earlier, I mentioned Internet Explorer on the Windows 8 desktop. This version can add more flexibility than is available in the app version of Internet Explorer 10. You open Internet Explorer on the desktop by clicking or tapping the *Desktop* tile on the Start screen. You will then see Internet Explorer pinned to the Taskbar that runs along the bottom of the screen.

Unlike the app version of Internet Explorer, this desktop version supports browser plug-ins and toolbars and is also much better if you have a great many Internet favorites that you like to visit.

It works in the same way as previous versions of Internet Explorer and other Internet browsers, and some users may prefer to use this version of the web browser.

 If you are viewing a web page in the Internet Explorer app, you can open it in the full desktop browser by clicking the *wrench* icon in the App Bar, then selecting *View on the Desktop* from the options that appear.

Using Windows Live Mail

While Windows 8 does include a Mail app, some people want a more fully featured program that works more like Microsoft Outlook that you might use at work. Windows Live Mail is a great free alternative to Outlook that you can download from *http://download.live.com* or from the Windows Store. Windows Live Mail is part of the excellent Windows Essentials Suite that includes Windows Photo Gallery, which I will discuss in Chapter 6.

 Remember that you can't install additional desktop software on a Windows tablet.

Windows Live Mail (Figure 2-5) runs on the Windows Desktop and includes many of the features present in Microsoft Outlook (which you might use at work), while at the same time being very easy to use.

Figure 2-5. Windows Live Mail

There are five tabs across the top of the program in a *ribbon*. This is where you control the program:

- **File** is a tab you will probably not need, but here you can customize the options for the program or add and remove email accounts.
- **Home** is the main tab that includes all the functions you need to create, send, and receive email.
- **Folders** is where you can organize your email by moving and copying them, and by creating folders.
- **View** is where you can change how email is displayed in Windows Live Mail.
- **Accounts** is where you can manage and tell Windows Live Mail about your existing email account.

 If you have used a Microsoft Account to sign into Windows 8, Windows Live Mail will automatically recognize this and configure your email account for you.

Step by Step: Setting Up Email in Windows Live Mail

1. Click/Touch the *Accounts* tab on the Ribbon.
2. Click/Touch the *Email* Button.
3. Enter the email address and password for your account and your name.
4. Click/Touch *Next* and Windows Live Mail will now download your email (Figure 2-6; this may take some time if you have a lot of email).

Summary

It is very easy to get online with Windows 8, and if you use a Microsoft Account to sign into your computer, then Windows 8 takes all the strain out of setting up and configuring your email account, calendar, and more. Even if you use a Gmail, Yahoo!, or other account, it is quick and simple to set up your accounts in the People app.

If you want more control, the Windows Essentials Suite is an excellent package with some fantastic programs in it for blogging, photo editing, messaging, and more, and you can install it on desktop and laptop computers.

Now that you're online, in Chapter 3 I'll show you how you can share your files, photos, and more with friends and family, both inside your home and on the Internet.

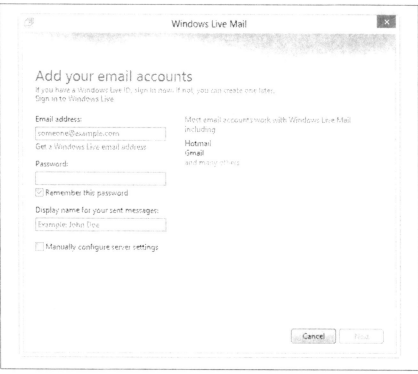

Figure 2-6. Setting up an email account in Windows Live

Sharing Your Files, Photos, Music, and Video

Sharing our lives and experiences online is becoming ever more popular as digital cameras and smartphones reduce in price and improve with every new model. Add to this social networking websites and instant messaging and it's easy to see why hundreds of millions of people are sharing things with friends and family online.

You might want to share files and memories with members of your own family and friends. Windows 8 is the most connected operating system Microsoft has ever produced, with features that are built in to make it simpler than ever to share files, photographs, music, and videos with family, friends, or the wider world through a blog or photo and video sharing website.

In Chapter 2, I showed you how to get online with Windows 8. Now let's look at how you can make sharing the best moments of your life enjoyable and problem-free.

Top Tips from This Chapter

1. Windows 8 includes features for sharing your files, photos, music, and videos, which you can access by clicking/touching *Share* in the Charms Menu.

2. You can share your files and even printers with other computers running Windows 8 or Windows 7 by setting up a HomeGroup.

3. You can share pictures, music, and video with non-Windows devices by turning on the Media Sharing feature in Windows 8.

The Windows 8 Sharing Tool

Windows 8 includes a new sharing tool that can be selected at any time from the *Charms Menu*. If you are looking at a picture, file, video, or other type of content that you want to share with other people, click/touch *Share* and you will be shown a list of apps that you can share this content with instantly. This list will vary depending on what apps you have installed (Figure 3-1).

Figure 3-1. The Share Menu options in the Charms Menu

This is where the real power of social apps comes into play and where apps that you can download from the Windows 8 Store can be much better and easier to use than visiting websites in Internet Explorer.

In Chapter 4, I will show you how to find and install apps in Windows 8, but for now, let me explain how Windows 8 sharing works and why using apps can be better than visiting a website.

Let's say, for example, that you have photos that you want to share on Facebook or a video you want to upload to YouTube.

In earlier versions of Windows, you would open Internet Explorer or another web browser, go to the website, log in, and upload them. However, if you have a compatible app installed in Windows 8 for these websites—let's say, a YouTube app—you view the video you want to share, open the Charms Menu, click/touch *Share*, and you will see the YouTube app appear in the list of compatible sharing apps.

Clicking/touching this app will automatically share the video with the app, and therefore on the website as well, with a minimum of fuss.

Sharing with Other People in Your Home

While Windows 8 makes it easy for you to share photos, videos, and more with friends and family on the Internet, it makes it just as easy to share things with people in your home on other computers. It does this using a *HomeGroup*.

You can find the settings for the HomeGroup by Clicking *Settings* in the Charms menu and then clicking *Change PC Settings*. The HomeGroup options are near the bottom of the PC Settings panel (Figure 3-2).

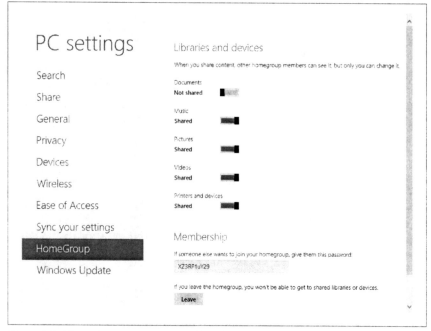

Figure 3-2. HomeGroup options in Windows 8

Here, you will see switches making it easy to share *Documents, Music, Pictures,* and *Videos* from this computer. Each computer in a HomeGroup can be configured differently so that, for example, a computer that's used in a home office might not share its Documents.

You can also share printers and other devices plugged into your computer. This makes it easy for people to be able to print documents or access other hardware (e.g., scanners or external hard disks) remotely, though the computer these are physically plugged into will need to be switched on.

 If you have a wireless printer, this can be accessed directly by other computers and won't need to be shared using Homegroup. I will show you how to set up printers in Chapter 7.

Sharing with Other Media Devices

Below the options for choosing what you want to share from your Windows 8 computer, you will see an option to *Allow all devices on the network such as TVs and game consoles to play my shared content*, but what does this mean?

Many devices in the home can now share content such as music and video even though they don't run Microsoft Windows. You might have a games console such as an Xbox 360 or a Wii U, an Internet-connected Smart TV, or an Internet radio. If you turn this option on, then all of these devices will be able to access your shared content—provided that they also have this feature enabled.

The advantage of this is that you can, for example, play your music library from your computer on your Internet radio in the garden, or watch videos you have stored on your computer on your living room TV.

Creating and Joining HomeGroups

Any computer running Windows 7 or Windows 8 can join a HomeGroup. You can find the Homegroup options in PC Settings under the *Homegroup* section. You can create a HomeGroup by turning the feature on, and you will be shown a password that will need to be entered on other computers when they join the HomeGroup.

If a HomeGroup has already been created on another computer, you will see a *Join* button. Click/touch or tap this and you can click/touch or tap where you will be prompted to enter the HomeGroup password. You can find this password in the HomeGroup settings on the computer the HomeGroup was created on.

If you no longer wish for a computer to be a member of a HomeGroup, you can also leave the HomeGroup by clicking/tapping the *Leave* button.

Connecting Windows 8 and Your Xbox 360

If you have an Xbox 360 console in your home, you can connect your Windows 8 computer to it. This gives you the advantage of being able to enjoy your music, photos, and videos on your TV.

Connecting to Your Xbox 360 Using the Xbox Companion App

You can connect your Windows 8 computer to your Xbox 360 console through the *Xbox Companion* App (Figure 3-3), which you can download for free from the Windows Store. I'll show you how to download and install apps in the next chapter.

Figure 3-3. Downloading and installing the Xbox Companion App

The Xbox Companion app (Figure 3-4) allows you to control your Xbox 360 console remotely from your Windows 8 computer. This includes being able to manage your Xbox Live account settings and games easily and using a Windows 8 tablet as a remote gaming control for the Xbox console.

Figure 3-4. Setting up the Xbox Companion App

When you first start the Xbox Companion App, you will be asked to make your Xbox 360 console available. You do this on the Xbox console itself from the Dashboard by opening *Settings*, then *Console Settings*, then *Xbox Companion* and changing the status to *Available*.

Changing this status setting will make sure that Windows 8 can detect the Xbox console.

To connect your Windows 8 computer to your Xbox 360 console, you will need to be logged in to both the computer and the Xbox using the same Microsoft account (your Xbox Live account).

Connecting to Your Xbox 360 Using Windows Media Center

When you connect your Xbox 360 console to your computer using the Windows Media Center software on your desktop or laptop computer, you can share your pictures, music, and videos with the console and enjoy it on your TV.

To do this, you will need Windows Media Center installed on your computer. You can check by going to the All Apps view where, if Media Center is installed, it will appear in the *Windows Accessories* section. If you don't have Media Center installed, it is a chargeable extra that you can buy by searching for *Add Features* at the Start screen and selecting *Add Features to Windows 8* from the Settings search results.

You will need to buy an upgrade to Windows 8, which you can do by clicking the *I want to buy a product key online* button, which will upgrade you to the full version of Windows 8 Pro with Media Center (Figure 3-5).

To connect your Xbox 360 console to your Windows 8 computer using Windows Media Center, start Windows Media Center from the *Video* panel on your Xbox 360 Dashboard and follow the simple instructions.

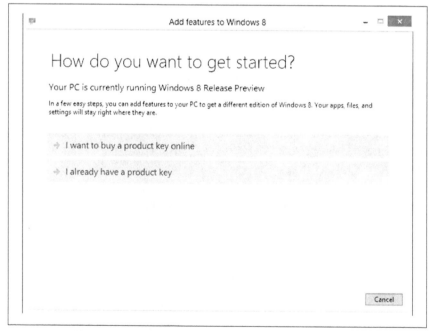

Figure 3-5. Adding features to Windows 8

If you do not have the full version of Windows 8 Pro with Media Center, you can share your pictures, music, and videos with an Xbox 360 console by turning on the *Allow all devices on the network such as TVs and game consoles to play my shared content* setting in *HomeGroup* from PC Settings.

Connecting to Other Devices in Your Home

While you can use HomeGroup to share files and printers between other Windows 7 and Windows 8 computers in your home, and you can use the Xbox Companion App or Windows Media Center to connect to an Xbox 360 console, you can also connect your Windows 8 computer to other networked devices in your home. These could include a USB hard disk plugged into your Internet router or a wireless printer. There are a couple of ways that you can do this.

Connecting to Devices from the Charms Menu

Open the Charms menu and select *Devices* to see other hardware devices you can use and access from your Windows 8 computer. Not all devices will appear in this view, so you may find that the specific device you want to use isn't displayed, but this is a good way to connect quickly to hardware that's fully compatible with Windows 8 features.

Connecting to Devices from File Explorer

To connect to other networked devices in your home, open *Desktop* from the Start screen and on the Taskbar that runs along the bottom of the desktop, click/touch the yellow folder icon to open *File Explorer*. Once File Explorer is open on your desktop, look in its left-hand panel, where you will see a link for *Network*.

Click/Touch this link to see all compatible network devices in your home. This will include other computers running Windows and any compatible computers such as Macs, networked media devices such as Internet radios, and any additional hardware such as a USB hard disk plugged into your Internet router if your router supports this feature (Figure 3-6).

You can access external hardware and computers directly from this panel to share files between them and your Windows 8 computer. Not all hardware devices will appear, however, and some that appear might not allow you to share files this way. For example, if you have a non-Windows 8 tablet such as an iPad or Android device, you will probably not be able to share files

Figure 3-6. Viewing network devices in Windows 8

wirelessly. You might need to physically plug that tablet in to a desktop or laptop computer to copy files to it.

Summary

Sharing is becoming an ever more important and increasingly central part of our everyday lives. In Windows 8, it's easier than ever before to share your files, photos, music, and videos between Windows 8 apps and websites. If you have other hardware in your home that you want to share files with, perhaps to create a backup of your files, this is easy to do as well. I will show you how to create backups in Chapter 11.

I've mentioned already that some of the features I have talked about in this chapter require you to get apps from the Windows Store, and in Chapter 4, I'll show you how to use the Windows Store; how you can find, download, and install apps; and how you can manage them on your computer.

Downloading and Using Apps and Programs

To get the very best out of using your computer, you will want to install apps and programs. These can be anything from games to file and photo sharing and technical or financial apps, which are all now found in the new Windows Store. You can access the *Store* from the Start screen.

It is the strength and variety of apps and programs that make Windows flexible and powerful, and can allow people to use their computers for whatever tasks they wish from entertainment to work.

While your Windows 8 computer comes with some great apps, including Mail, Photos, Music, and Messaging, you will probably want to install more apps onto it, and even programs that run on the Windows desktop, especially if you already have software from a previous PC that you want to use and that you are comfortable with at this time.

Windows 8 makes it easier than ever before to find software with the new *Store*, which can be launched from the Start screen. *All* Windows 8 apps can be found here; you can't get them from anywhere else. Not only does this make apps simple to find, but it also makes the process of paying for them and downloading them much more secure because Microsoft scans all apps for malware.

Top Tips from This Chapter

1. The Windows Store is the central and safe place to find apps and programs.
2. You can drag and rearrange Tiles and icons on the Start screen to make them easier to find and organize.

3. You can view apps and desktop programs side by side, which can make working easier.

Using the Windows Store

You open the Windows Store by clicking the *Store* icon on the Start screen. It is arranged into app categories including Games, Entertainment, and Books & Reference. There are also quick links for the most popular and highest-rated apps (Figure 4-1).

Figure 4-1. The new Windows Store

You can find out more information on an app by clicking it. Here you will see the main information about the app in a panel on the left, and on the right, links to view the app's Overview, Details, and Reviews.

On the bottom left, you will see a section called "This app has permission to use," where the Store will tell what personal information on your computer, if any, the app will want access to. Why is this important? Your personal information is of great economic value to companies. They want to know more about you so that they can directly target advertising at you and they may sell the information they hold about you to other companies.

If you allow an app access to information such as your email or Facebook account, you are potentially giving it huge volumes of very private information about you that you would otherwise not share. Always be careful in choosing apps, and do not install any that request access to information they should not ordinarily need.

Below this is an age rating for the app. This can be especially useful if you have young children who use your computer to play games.

You can install an app by clicking/touching the *Install* button, though you will have to register a credit or debit card with the Store to buy any apps that are not free.

At all stages while browsing apps, a *back* button will appear in the top left corner of your screen so you can return to the Store main page. You can also return to the main store page by clicking/touching *Home* from the App Bar.

 You can often find extra options and controls in an app by opening the Charms menu and clicking/tapping the *Settings* icon. If available in that app, extra options will appear in the top right of your screen.

Updating Apps in Windows 8

Occasionally, the apps you install on your Windows 8 computer will be up-dated with new features and fixes. The Windows Store will inform you of this by displaying the number of current updates on the Store Live Tile (Figure 4-2).

When updates are available for apps and when you open the Store app, you will see a notification in the top right of your screen concerning how many updates are available. Clicking this notification will allow you to install all the updates quickly and simply.

It is usually a good idea to install app updates because some might be security related and fix flaws that could make you vulnerable to criminals or that could make your copy of Windows unstable. Some may also add new features to the app.

Making Tiles Smaller and Larger

Some Tiles can be made larger and smaller, to display less or more information. You might want to make the Mail tile smaller, for example, so that it only shows you the number of new emails and not the senders and subjects (if perhaps other people can read over your shoulder), or you may have a news

Figure 4-2. The Store Tile tells you when app updates are available

Tile that when made larger shows you additional information about current events (you can see an example of different sizes of Tile in Figure 4-3).

Figure 4-3. Different sized tiles

You can make a Tile larger or smaller by *touching it and dragging downwards* with your finger or *right-clicking* it with your mouse. From the App Bar, you can then click/touch the *Smaller* or *Larger* button. If you do not see a smaller or larger option, then the tile you have selected cannot be resized.

You can also turn the Live Tile off for an app completely, perhaps for privacy reasons, by selecting *Turn Live Tile Off* from the App Bar when you have selected it. This prevents the Tile from displaying information such as details of emails, photos, or calendar appointments.

Organizing App Icons on the Start Screen

When you install new apps on your Windows 8 computer, or create an Internet Favorite in the Internet Explorer App, these will all appear as tiles on the far right of the Start screen. This can cause your Start screen to become cluttered quite quickly, making it very difficult to find what you are looking for. As you add Tiles to the Start screen, it expands to the right and can get very large.

You can move these Tiles around to organize them, and even hide them completely from the main view to help keep them organized.

If you are using a mouse, remember to look for the scroll bar at the bottom of your screen. You can drag this to move left and right on the Start screen. You can also use your mouse scroll wheel to pan left and right on the Start screen.

You might want to reorganize the tiles on your Start screen so that all the apps, websites, and programs you use regularly have their Tiles on the far left of your screen, to make them easier to access. You might also install software such as Microsoft Office and want to hide the extra programs it installs, such as the Office Picture Viewer.

Arranging the Start Screen Step by Step

To arrange your apps, websites, and programs on the Start screen (see Figure 4-4), follow these quick steps:

- Click/Touch and then hold, drag, and drop tiles around the Start screen to rearrange them using either your finger or your mouse.
- Hold a tile between groups to create a new group again using either your finger or your mouse. Drop it on the vertical bar that appears.
- Remove a tile from the Start screen by touching it and dragging downwards, or *right-clicking* with your mouse, and then click/touch *Unpin from Start* from the App Bar.

If you unpin a Tile from the Start screen, it will be removed, but you will still be able to access it when you want to. I will show you how to do this later in this chapter.

Figure 4-4. Working with Live Tiles

Arranging Groups of Tiles

I mentioned previously that you can create new groups of Tiles by dragging a Tile to the space between groups and, when you see a vertical bar appear, dropping the Tile. You can also name and rearrange whole groups of Tiles simply and quickly.

You can give groups of Tiles names by zooming out of the Start screen (see Figure 4-5). You can do this in one of three ways:

- Make an outward pinch zoom gesture with your fingers
- *Click* with your mouse in the very bottom right corner of the Start screen
- Hold the *Ctrl* key on your keyboard and use your mouse wheel to zoom out

You can now drag and rearrange whole groups of tiles to arrange them how best suits you. You can also give groups names, such as "Websites" or perhaps "Desktop Programs" by *right-clicking* on or *touching and dragging downwards* on an app group.

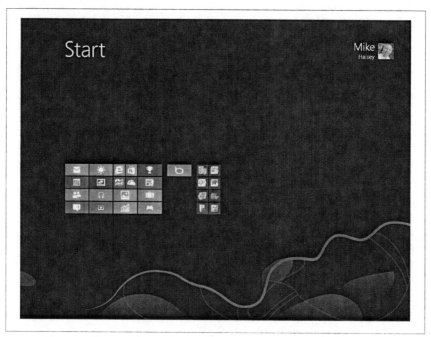

Figure 4-5. Zooming out of the Start screen

Viewing All Your Installed Apps and Programs

I showed you earlier how you can hide apps and programs from your Start screen. But surely if you hide them, then you can't use them? Fortunately, it's easy to see all of the apps and programs that you have installed on your computer at any time.

To see hidden apps and programs, open the app bar from the Start screen and click/touch the *All Apps* button. Here, you will be able to see all the apps and programs that are installed on your computer (Figure 4-6). Programs are organized into groups as you would see in the Start Menu in previous versions of Windows.

You cannot rearrange apps and programs in the All Apps view into different groups, but it is easy to see all the software you have installed. Remember, this view can also expand outward to the right, so you may need to swipe left and right to view everything. Again, if you are using a mouse, a scroll bar will appear at the bottom of the screen.

Figure 4-6. The All Apps view

Don't Have Too Much Software Installed

Sometimes it's easy to have lots of apps and programs installed on your Windows 8 computer. Perhaps you have downloaded apps to try them, and you later decide you don't want to use them.

You should always keep the number of apps and programs on your computer to a minimum. Having too much software installed can cause Windows 8 to become unstable over time and it can also make it much more difficult to find the app or program you want to use.

I would also recommend against installing any app or program that duplicates a function that is already part of Windows; for example, CD or DVD burning software, mapping software, or another web browser. Each extra piece of software just adds to the overall complexity of the computer, and with complexity can come instability, as I write about in my book *Troubleshoot and Optimize Windows 8 Inside Out*.

Switching Between Running Apps and Programs

Apps in Windows 8 run full screen by default, but you will want to switch between them and use more than one at a time. There are several different ways to switch between running apps and programs on your computer. If you are using touch, then dragging your finger in from the left of your screen will drag the previously seen app onto the screen.

With your keyboard, you can use the *WindowsKey+Tab* keypress to switch between running apps or the *Alt+Tab* key combination to switch between all running app and desktop programs. The WindowsKey is in the bottom right of your keyboard with the Windows logo on it, and Tab can be found near the top left of the keyboard.

To switch between apps using the keyboard, hold down the Alt or Windows Key and keep pressing Tab until you get to the program you want. The currently running apps and programs will appear as thumbnail images at either the left side of the screen or in the center of the screen.

Viewing Two Apps Side by Side

You can also view apps (and even the desktop) side by side on your screen. To view apps side by side, grab the app at the top of the screen with your finger or mouse and drag it toward the center of the screen. You will see that it changes to a thumbnail image. When you drag this thumbnail to the left or right of the screen, you will see a vertical bar appear; this signifies that dropping the app there will dock it in a panel to that side of the window (Figure 4-7).

Figure 4-7. Viewing two apps side by side

You can now return to the Start screen and run another app. This second app will appear, filling the main portion of the screen with your *docked* app sitting at the left or right of it.

 You can also select another running app by holding down the *WindowsKey* on your keyboard and pressing the *Tab* key to cycle through thumbnail images of running apps. For desktop programs, use the key combination *Shift+Tab* instead.

You can change which app fits the small window and which takes the main focus of your screen by dragging the bar that separates them left and right. You can also drag this bar to the far edge of the screen to remove the smaller app from view completely.

Viewing Two Desktop Windows Side by Side

You can also view desktop programs side by side (Figure 4-8). This can be very useful for comparing two documents or web pages. To do this, click/touch or touch and hold the top of the desktop program window and drag it to the far left or right of your screen. You will see a shadow appear when your mouse touches the screen edge to show you that the program will be resized to fill exactly half of your screen's width and docked to one side of the screen.

Drag your other program to the opposite side of the screen and it will fill the other half of your screen's width. You can return them to their original shape and size by dragging them away from the side of the screen in the same way that you put them there.

To compare two web pages side by side when you have multiple tabs open in the desktop version of Internet Explorer, drag an individual tab out of the window and it will then appear in its own Internet Explorer Window. These can then be snapped to the left and right of the screen.

Uninstalling Apps and Programs in Windows 8

You won't always want to have every app or program installed forever. You may, for example, have installed something just to try it out or because you thought it was what you were looking for, only to discover later that it is an app or program you don't want to keep.

You can uninstall any app or program from the Start screen or the All Apps view by *touching it and dragging downwards* or *right-clicking* on it. In the app bar, you will see an uninstall option.

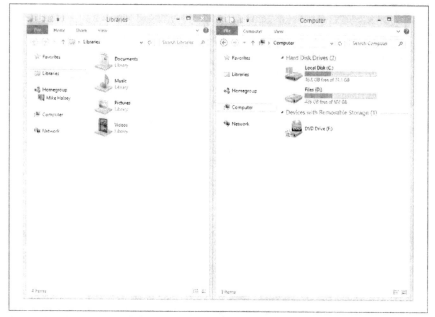

Figure 4-8. Viewing two desktop programs side by side

If you are uninstalling a desktop program, you will be taken to the *Programs and Features* window on the desktop. Here, you should click the program you wish to uninstall and on the toolbar near the top of the window, you will see an option to uninstall the program.

Summary

There are many cool ways to work with apps and programs in Windows 8, and the new Windows Store will help keep malware off your computer as well as making it much simpler to find the software you want. Security is still important, though, and I will show you how to keep your computer safe in Chapter 10.

It's well worth spending some time arranging your apps and programs into groups on the Start screen, because this will make it much easier to find things later on.

Now that I've shown you how to use and work with apps and programs in Windows 8, in Chapter 5, I'll show you how you can enjoy playing your music and videos.

Watching and Listening to Your Videos and Music

As you accumulate your collections of digital music and videos, you'll want to enjoy this content on your Windows 8 computer. Windows 8 comes with some excellent apps that make it easy to enjoy and organize your media.

Top Tips from This Chapter

1. Windows 8 comes with apps for playing both music and videos.
2. When looking at links in apps that have a down arrow to their right, you can click/touch the arrow for more options.
3. If you have a desktop computer, a laptop, or a Windows 8 Pro tablet, you can also use Windows Media Player to sort, organize, and play your music and video collection.

Watching Your Videos in Windows 8

You can play your videos in the *Videos* App, which you can access from the Start screen. When you first open the Videos App, you will be presented with a display showing videos that you can watch or purchase online (Figure 5-1).

To view your own videos, you should pan left either with a swipe of your finger or by moving your mouse to the bottom of the screen, where you will find the scroll bar. You can also use the scroll wheel on your mouse to move around left and right in Apps.

Your videos display will show you your most recently added videos. To view all of your videos, click/touch the *My Videos* link at the top of this section to be taken to a new view where you will see all of your videos.

Figure 5-1. The Videos App

Click or tap the back arrow in the top left of the screen at any time to return to the previous page.

There are several different ways to organize your videos. Near the top left of the screen, you can click/touch on the *Date Added* link to view your video library in different ways, such as *A to Z* or by *duration*. You can click/touch on any video to play it and you will see play controls appear on the screen, which will fade when you don't touch the screen or move the mouse for a few seconds, but that will reappear when you do touch the screen or move the mouse.

At any time, you can *right-click* with your mouse or swipe upward with your finger from the bottom of the screen to open more controls on the App Bar.

You may have videos stored in different folders on your computer or perhaps in a different location, such as an external USB hard disk. To play files in different locations, open the App Bar and click/touch *Open File*. This will open the folder view where you can look through all your files and folders to view any videos (Figure 5-2). This also applies to the Music App in Windows 8.

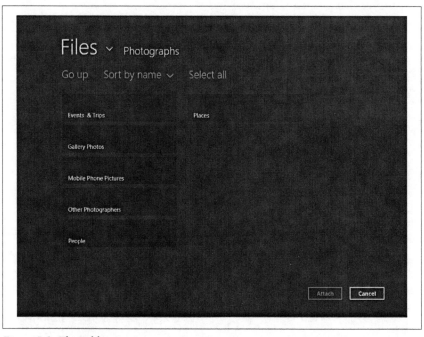

Figure 5-2. The Folder view

Using the Folder View

The *Open File* view allows you to view any files you have stored, not just on your own computer, but also in compatible Internet services such as Microsoft SkyDrive. You can click/touch on any link that has a view. For example, clicking the *Files* link will display folders, including your documents, pictures, and even your entire computer and network. Below this are links to other available locations such as SkyDrive.

You move around folders in this view by clicking on them. If you want to move up a folder location, click/touch the *Go Up* link. Videos can be opened and played by clicking or touching them.

Playing Your Music in Windows 8

The Music App is also opened from the Start screen and looks and works in a very similar way to the Video App. When you first open it, you are shown music that you can purchase online. Swipe left to view your own music collection (or move your mouse to the bottom of the screen and a scroll bar will appear that you can drag left).

The Music App will show you your most recently added music first. Click/ touch the *My Music* link to view the whole music collection on your computer. Here you can arrange your music by *Songs*, *Albums*, or *Artists* by clicking the links on the left side of the screen (Figure 5-3). You can also view any *Playlists* you have created. More on creating playlists will follow shortly.

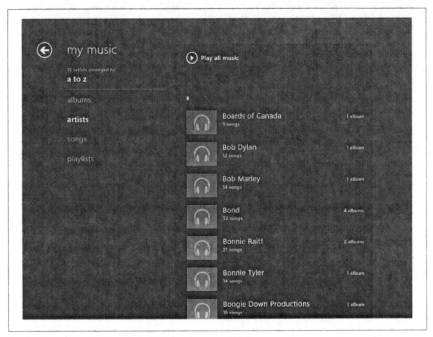

Figure 5-3. Viewing your music collection

When you are looking at the Playlists view, you can click/ touch the + button to create a new playlist.

You can click/touch the *Date Added* link at the top left of the screen to sort and arrange your music in different ways, including by *genre* or by *A to Z*.

When you click/touch on an album, the screen will dim and your selected album will be highlighted in the center of the screen (Figure 5-4). Here, you can click/touch on an individual track to play; when you select the track, a *Play* button will appear. Alternatively, you can click/touch the *Play* button under the album cover artwork to play the whole album.

At any time, you can also click/touch *Add to Now Playing* to add the track to the end of the current music playlist. As with the Video App, playback controls will appear on screen and will fade when you are not moving the mouse or touching the screen.

Figure 5-4. Playing music

 Open the App Bar at any time to display the play controls in the Music and Video Apps.

Using Windows Media Player

If you want more control over your music library and you are using a desktop computer, laptop, or Windows 8 Pro tablet, you can use Windows Media Player (Figure 5-5). You can start Windows Media Player by searching for **media** at the Start screen.

Figure 5-5. Windows Media Player

This software offers several advantages over the Music App, especially for people with large music collections. In the left panel are quick links to let you arrange and view your music by *Artist*, *Album*, or *Genre* and you can also view your *Videos* and *Pictures* here as well. Below these links are direct links to any other computers or network devices that are sharing pictures, music, and video on your network. This can include other computers and network storage.

Perhaps the best functionality with Windows Media Player is the advanced ability to control playlists. Click/Touch *Create Playlist* in the options bar that runs along the top of the window and you can create either a standard playlist or an auto playlist. Let me explain the difference.

When you create a Standard Playlist, it will appear in the left-side navigation panel in Windows Media Player. You can drag and drop music onto this playlist using your mouse to add music to it.

Auto playlists, however, will automatically add music to the playlists depending on various criteria that you set (Figure 5-6). You can choose from a great many options here to create, for example, auto playlists of your most played music or even music tracks that you've never played.

Figure 5-6. Windows Media Player

If, at any time, you want to create an audio CD—perhaps to play in the car of your favorite music—you can do this by clicking the *Burn* link in the top right of the window and dragging and dropping the music tracks you want into the panel that appears. When you have selected the tracks you want, click/touch the *Start Burn* button to burn your audio CD (you will need a blank CD and a CD burner drive in your computer to do this).

Summary

The built-in apps for playing music and videos in Windows 8 are perfectly capable, although you might prefer to use an alternative player such as the excellent Zune Desktop software from Microsoft or, if you have an iPhone, iTunes software. If you are using a Windows 8 tablet, you won't be able to install these desktop software packages, but alternative music and video playing apps will be available in the Windows Store. See Chapter 4 for details of how to install apps and software.

In Chapter 6, I'll show you how you can view your pictures and photographs on your computer, how you can import images from a digital camera, how you can do basic editing on your photos, and then how to display them as show slideshows.

Importing, Viewing, and Editing Your Photographs and Videos

Photographs are an ever-important part of life, allowing us to relive precious moments or share in the experiences of our friends and family. Digital cameras have allowed us to take many more photographs than we could have with film cameras and to share them in new and exciting ways both with friends and family and also with the wider world. You can read more about how to share your digital photographs in Chapter 3.

While your digital camera will probably come with software that will enable you to import photos and organize them in different ways, Windows 8 includes many of these features as standard so that in many cases there's no need to install the additional software that came with your camera.

Top Tips from This Chapter

1. Windows Photo Gallery, free from Microsoft, includes some excellent photo-management and editing tools.
2. You can choose what happens when you plug a memory card into your computer through the *Default Programs* panel.
3. Tags can be added to photos to make them easier to find.

Importing Photos and Video from Your Digital Camera

You can import photos and video from your digital camera or camcorder in the same way, either by plugging your camera directly into your computer using a cable, or by removing the memory card from the camera and inserting it into a card reader built into or attached to the PC.

You can't import photos to all Windows 8 tablets, especially the consumer tablets. This is because many of these tablets don't support external devices and hardware in the way desktop computers do. If you are thinking of buying a Windows 8 tablet, you should ask if it supports memory cards.

When you insert your memory card into your PC or plug your camera in via a USB or other cable, an alert will appear in the top right of your screen saying that Windows 8 has found your *storage device* (Figure 6-1). Click/Touch this alert to tell Windows that you want to use this device and then click/touch the *Import Photos and Videos* option that appears.

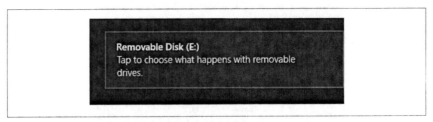

Removable Disk (E:)
Tap to choose what happens with removable drives.

Figure 6-1. Choose what to do with a memory card

The Photo and Video import wizard will then appear and automatically select all the photos and videos on the camera or memory card for import (Figure 6-2). By default, it will create a folder in your *Pictures* library named for the date (year, month, day) you have imported the photos, but you can rename the file. To change the name of the folder your photos and video will be imported to, perhaps from *2012-06-14* to *Amsterdam, October 2012*, click/touch the white box at the bottom of the screen to edit the folder name.

By default, Windows 8 will import every photo and video on the card and you can see what is selected because a small check icon will appear in the top right of each thumbnail image displayed. You can select and remove items from being imported by tapping them.

 If not all of your photos and videos are appearing on the screen, scroll to the right to view more of them, as only so many will be displayed on the screen at one time.

When you are ready to import photos and videos to your computer, click/touch the *Import* button in the bottom right of the screen to start the import process. When this is complete, you will be asked if you want to open the

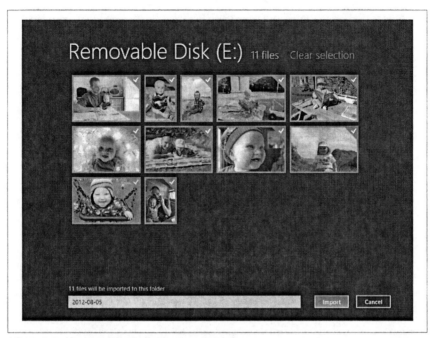

Figure 6-2. The Photo and Video Import Wizard

album you have created to view the imported photos and videos on your computer.

The imported photos will not be deleted from your memory card or camera during this import process, so you will have to delete them afterward, either using File Explorer on the Windows 8 desktop or the camera settings.

Advanced Photo and Video Import Using Windows Photo Gallery

Sometimes you want more control over your photos—certainly when it comes to editing them—and this is where Microsoft's Windows Photo Gallery software is useful. You can download it as part of the Windows Essentials Suite from *http://download.live.com*.

With Windows Photo Gallery installed on your Windows 8 computer (it won't install on a Windows 8 tablet), you get much more control over the photo and video import process.

To import photos using Windows Photo Gallery, open the Photo Gallery software and click/tap the *File* tab in the top left of the window. From the options that appear, click/tap *Import photos and videos*.

If you are automatically taken to the Windows 8 Photo and Video Importer App, search for *Default* at the Start screen and run the *Default Programs* option that appears. Click/Touch *Change autoplay settings* in the page that appears and change the *Camera Storage* option to either *Import Photos and Videos (Windows Photo Gallery)* or *Ask me every time*.

A new import window will now appear where you have more choices. Let's look at each of these in turn (Figure 6-3).

Figure 6-3. The Photo and Video Import Wizard (Windows Photo Gallery)

Review, Organize, and Group Items to Import

This option will group your photos by the date they were taken. This allows you to split photos taken on a longer trip or vacation into different folders to keep them separate. At the top of each group, as you can see in Figure 6-4, you can enter a name for that group. Let's say you were on a European road trip. On the first day you were in the Netherlands; on the second and third days, you were in Germany; and on the fourth day, you visited Poland. Because the Import Wizard splits the photos into groups sorted by date, you can label each group of photos appropriately.

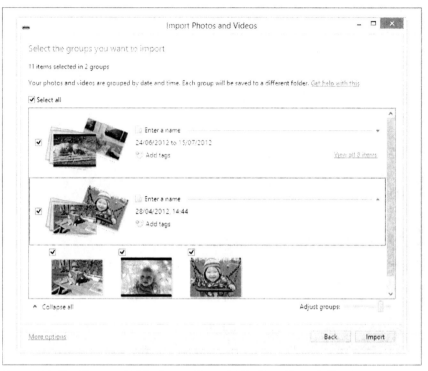

Figure 6-4. *The Photo and Video Import Wizard (Windows Photo Gallery)*

 If the photo groups are not appearing correctly, you can use the *Adjust groups* slider in the bottom right of the window to create more or fewer groups, again arranged by date and time.

You can also select which photos and videos you wish to import by checking and unchecking the boxes in the top left of each thumbnail image. There are three different types of box you can check.

1. The *Select all* check box will select every photo and video for import.
2. You can check the box to the left of each group to select all of the items in that group.
3. You can select photos and videos individually using the check box to left of its thumbnail image.

In the bottom left of the import window is a *More options* link. This provides additional functionality, such as choosing the default import folder location for pictures and videos, the default naming convention for new photos and videos, whether you want Windows Photo Gallery to automatically rotate images so they are correctly oriented, and if you want photos and videos to be automatically deleted from your camera or memory card on import to Windows.

Import All New Items Now

The second option at the main import screen is much more straightforward. It will import every photo and video from the camera or memory card. You will be prompted to give a name for the photos, perhaps *Dusseldorf, October 2012*, and this will be the name of the folder, and each imported photo and video will be labelled according to this name.

Additionally, you can click/touch the *Add tags* link to add key words to the photos and videos that can make them easier to search for and organize. For example, you might add the words *holiday* and *Germany*. You can then search for *Germany* in Windows Photo Gallery or File Explorer to bring up all photos taken in that country. You should separate all individual tags with a semicolon (;).

 If the photo and video import options aren't appearing when you plug your camera or memory card into your computer, open the *Photos* app and from the App Bar select *Import*. Here, you will be able to tell Windows 8 where to import your pictures from.

Viewing Your Photos in Windows 8

The *Photos* App, accessible from the Start screen, is your main location for viewing your digital photo collection (Figure 6-5). This allows you not only to view pictures and photos stored on your computer, but also ones that you have stored in Internet services such as SkyDrive, Facebook, and Flickr.

The main photos view shows your photos and folders as a series of panels that you can click/touch to open. These panels run left to right across your screen; if you are using a mouse with your computer, you will see a scroll bar appear at the bottom of the screen that you can click/touch and drag left and right. You can also use the scroll wheel on your mouse to move left and right in the Music App.

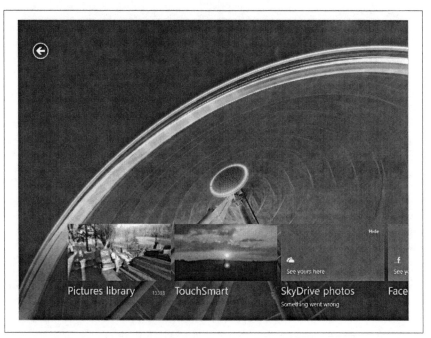

Figure 6-5. The Photos App in Windows 8

 You can hide some photo locations from the main screen of the Photos App by clicking the *Hide* link in the top right of their thumbnail image. For example, you might want to hide *Flickr* because you do not use this Internet service to store any photos.

At any time, you can move back a folder by clicking the back arrow in the top left of the screen.

Viewing Photo Slideshows

You can show slideshows of photos in the currently displayed folder by opening the App Bar and clicking the *Slideshow* button. This will automatically display a slideshow of all the currently selected photos, which you can cancel at any time by tapping the screen or pressing the *Esc* key on your keyboard.

If you want to share one or more photos by email or on the Internet, select them by either *right-clicking* each one with your mouse or by *tapping and pulling downwards* with your finger. Alternatively, you can open the App Bar and click/ touch the *Select All* button. You can now open the Charms Menu and click/touch *Share*. A list of compatible apps you can use to share your photos will appear; tap the appropriate app to share the photos.

Editing Your Photos in Windows Photo Gallery

The Photos App in Windows 8 doesn't support editing your photos and it's well worth looking through the Microsoft Store to find photo editing apps that you can use (Figure 6-6). If you see Adobe Photoshop Touch available, this is always an excellent purchase.

However, if you have downloaded the Windows Essentials Suite, Windows Photo Gallery offers some easy to use and really quite powerful photo editing tools. You can double-click/touch a picture to open it in editing mode and you will see that the Ribbon at the top of the window changes to an *Edit* tab. There there are many controls to choose from, but I want to detail the ones you are most likely to use.

Figure 6-6. Windows Photo Gallery

- The **Manage** section includes controls for rotating the image.
- The **Organize** section allows you to add and manage tags. These can be used to make it easier to search for specific images.
- The **Adjustments** panel is where the editing tools can be found.
  - *Auto adjust* will attempt to intelligently edit the brightness, contrast, rotation, and other aspects of the photograph.
  - *Crop* allows you to trim the image down to a smaller size, removing unwanted items from around the main focus of the picture.
  - *Red eye* will help remove the red eye effect caused by some cameras. You can click/touch on the red in people's eyes to have it intelligently removed.
  - *Fine Tune* gives you more control over the adjustments made by the *Auto adjust* feature.
  - **Revert to Original** is a very useful feature if you have made changes to a picture that you did not intend to make or that changed the photo in an unwelcome way. When you edit a photo using Windows Photo Gallery, a backup of the original image is made automatically. At any time, you can click/touch the *Revert to Original* button to restore that original image and undo any changes you have made.

Summary

Our photographs are very precious and we want to be able to enjoy and preserve them. Windows 8 includes some excellent features that enable us to import them from digital cameras and also to share your digital photographs with friends and family.

You may want to print out your photos, though, and in Chapter 7, I'll show you how to use printers and other external hardware with your Windows 8 computer.

Connecting To and Using Extra Hardware with Your Computer

In Chapter 6, I showed you how to import your digital photographs to your Windows 8 computer and how you can view them and perform some basic editing on them using Windows Live Photo Gallery. At some point, however, you might want to print some photographs or documents or connect your computer to external hardware. Let's start with printers.

Top Tips from This Chapter

1. Windows 8 can automatically detect and install wireless printers.
2. You can access network storage drives easily in File Explorer.
3. Windows 8 supports new multiscreen features including panoramic wallpapers.

Attaching and Using a Printer

Windows 8 can automatically detect and install printers, even ones that are on your home or work WiFi network. You might find that the first time you want to print something that the printer has already been automatically installed.

You can check if your printer (or other external hardware) is installed by opening *PC Settings* and clicking/touching the *Devices* section (Figure 7-1). You will see a list of all installed hardware in the top right side of the screen, and at the top of the list is an *Add a device* button that you can click/touch to add something that hasn't been installed already.

Figure 7-1. The Devices Panel in PC Settings

 To connect a wireless printer or other wireless network device to your home network, press the *WPS* button on both the printer and on your home Internet router to pair the devices. Check the documentation that came with your printer and router to see if this feature is supported on your devices and where the button is located.

When you click/touch the *Add a device* button, Windows 8 will search for devices connected directly to your computer via a cable and also for devices that are connected to your network. When Windows finds the device, it will appear in a list of new hardware, and Windows 8 will try to install it automatically.

 To help with installing printers, make sure your computer is connected to the Internet when you connect the printer, so that Windows 8 can download the necessary software to install the printer correctly.

Sometimes a printer does not automatically install, or perhaps doesn't install correctly. If this happens, then Windows 8 includes a utility to help you manage and reinstall the devices. This is called the *Devices and Printers* Panel (Figure 7-2), and you can open it by searching for *device* at the Start screen, which can be found in the *Settings* search results.

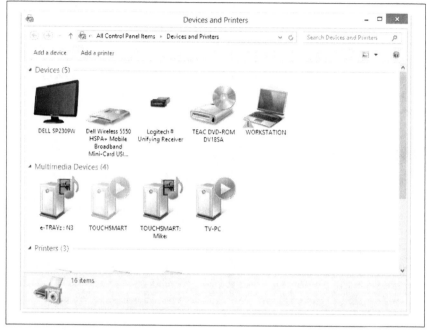

Figure 7-2. The Devices and Printers Panel

Sometimes, and this is possible with WiFi network printers that Windows 8 has installed incorrectly, you might need to remove a printer or other device before you can reinstall it. Look for it in the list of installed devices, and if it appears in the list, right-click (or tap and hold) it, and from the options that appear, select *Remove Device*.

You can now click/touch the *Add a Printer* link near the top left of the Devices and Printers panel and Windows 8 will automatically search for printers that are both attached to the computer or that are on your network.

Printers and other devices usually come with a CD or DVD containing software and drivers. If you put this disk in your computer's DVD or Blu-Ray drive, Windows 8 will ask you what you want to do. Select the *Run Setup* option to install your hardware.

The biggest difference between Windows 8 automatically installing printers and other devices and doing it yourself through the Devices and Printers Panel is that you can specify the correct driver to install, making sure that the hardware works correctly with your computer.

After you have selected the device to install, Windows 8 will ask if you want to install the device automatically or *Browse my computer for driver software*. It is this second option that you want to select. Make sure the driver CD that came with your hardware is in your DVD drive.

A *Browse* button will appear. Click/Touch this and navigate to the CD or DVD, where the drivers for your hardware can be found. Make sure you have checked the *Include subfolders* box in this panel so that Windows 8 searches the entire disk. When you are ready, click/touch the *Next* button to install your device.

Setting the Default Printer

If you have more than one printer, or perhaps if an error occurred when your printer was installed, you might find that when you try to print something, it's either not printing, printing on the wrong printer, or opening a "save" window on your screen instead. This happens because the *default* printer has not been set correctly.

To rectify this, open the *Devices and Printers* panel and then *right-click* (or tap and hold) on the printer you want to print from as the default printer. When options appear, click/touch *Set as default printer*. Every print job will now be sent to this printer on your computer.

Connecting to Network Storage and Devices

You might have network storage in your home that you want to be able to use with your Windows 8 computer. This can include USB hard disks that you plug into some Internet routers to provide shared storage and backup for people in your home. This can be especially useful for sharing files between different computers or for having a location away from your main computer to back up documents, music, pictures, and videos.

To access network computers and drives, click/touch *Desktop* from the Start screen and on the Taskbar that runs along the bottom of the desktop, click/touch the yellow folder icon to open File Explorer.

In the left-hand panel, as seen in Figure 7-3, you have quick links to your Favorite links, Libraries, HomeGroup, and Computer. At the bottom of this list is a *Network* link. Click/Touch this and File Explorer will show you all the available network computers and drives (remember, they need to be switched on to be visible).

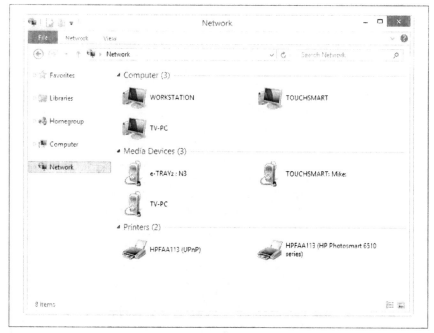

Figure 7-3. Accessing Network Storage in File Explorer

You can save network drives to your Start screen to give you easy access in the future. *Right-click* on a network drive and from the options that appear, click/touch *Pin to Start*. A shortcut link to the network storage will then be placed on your Start screen.

Using a Second Screen with Your Computer

Sometimes, and especially if you use your Windows 8 computer in a home office, you will want to attach a second screen to the computer. You can attach this to your computer via a VGA or DVI video cable (both of which are a D-shaped plug in either blue or white) or via an HDMI video lead. You should check the documentation that came with your computer to see what video ports are supported.

Windows 8 will automatically detect the second screen and perhaps even give you a picture on it straight away. You can also choose what is displayed on the second screen manually, however, by opening the Charms menu and clicking/ touching *Devices*. Now you should click/touch the *Second screen* option.

You now have four options for how to extend your screen to the second display (Figure 7-4).

Figure 7-4. Using a second screen with your Computer

- **PC Screen only** turns off the second screen.
- **Duplicate** will display the same thing on both screens.

- **Extend** will use both monitors together as a big, extended display.
- **Second Screen only** turns off the display on your main computer.

Whichever you choose, when you unplug the second screen, your computer's display will return to normal.

Customizing Your Multiscreen Display

Windows 8 includes some new features for multidisplay computers, including support for panoramic wallpapers on the desktop. To take advantage of this, *right-click* anywhere in empty space on the desktop and then click/touch *Personalize* from the options that appear.

At the bottom of the window that appears next, click/touch *Desktop background*. You will see some multiscreen wallpapers and you can click/touch the *Browse* button to use one or several of your own. When you have selected the correct image, click/touch the *Picture position* button at the bottom left of the panel and then click/touch *Span* from the available options (Figure 7-5).

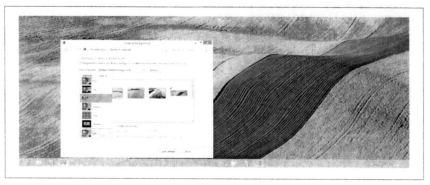

Figure 7-5. Setting a multiscreen wallpaper

Summary

Windows 8 is excellent at automatically detecting new hardware and installing it for you, even network printers that earlier versions of Windows haven't been able to do. It doesn't always get it right, but the controls available for you to fix problems are simply laid out and easy to use.

Moving on from connecting a second display to your computer, in Chapter 8, I'll show you how to set up and use your Windows 8 computer for work, so that you can be at your most productive.

Using Windows 8 for Work

Whether it's for work, college, or personal finance, Windows has always been the choice for being productive and getting things done. In Chapter 4, I showed you how you can snap two desktop windows side by side, which is a great way to compare two documents, and it's a feature that I use all the time.

There is much more that you can do with the desktop, though, and I'll show you how in this chapter. What's more, almost every version of Windows 8 comes with a free copy of Microsoft Office, either the Starter edition that you will find on desktops, laptops, and Windows 8 Pro tablets, or a more extensive yet still free version on Windows 8 consumer tablets.

Top Tips from This Chapter

1. The free Office Starter that comes with Windows 8 is suitable for many of the things home users will want to do in Word and Excel.
2. The Ribbon can be operated by touch and its tabs group similar functions together.
3. The Mobility Center has tools that can dramatically extend the battery life of a laptop or tablet.

Using Microsoft Office in Windows 8

As I've said in the introduction to this chapter, there are different versions of Office provided with your Windows 8 computer depending on what version of Windows 8 you have. I'll discuss the two different versions later in this chapter.

Microsoft Office is based around the company's *Ribbon* interface, which was first seen in Office 2007. This is an alternative way to access a program's features to the older-style drop-down menus. If you're not used to it, then test out some of the desktop programs supplied with Windows 8, including File Explorer, Paint, and WordPad. These all include the Ribbon. I will show you how to use the Ribbon shortly.

Microsoft Office Web Apps

Windows 8 on desktops and laptops doesn't come with a version of Microsoft Office installed, but you might see links to the *Office Web Apps*. You can find them on the Internet at *http://office.microsoft.com/web-apps*. These are based on Microsoft's new look for their latest version of Office and includes Word (Figure 8-1) and Excel. They look slightly different but are still based around the Ribbon interface.

Figure 8-1. Microsoft Word 2013

There are no limits to using the free version of the Office Web Apps, but you will need a live Internet connection to be able to use them. You will probably find that the web apps do almost everything you need in terms of a basic word processor and spreadsheet.

Using Microsoft Office on Windows 8 Tablets

If you have bought a Windows 8 tablet, you might find a more comprehensive version of Office installed. The programs here are still feature-limited versions of the full Office suite, but they include Word, Excel, PowerPoint (for making presentations), and OneNote (the note taking program that works very well on touch screens).

These versions cannot be upgraded to the full version of Office but, like the Starter edition, should meet most of your needs and they also support all of the formatting from the full Office apps.

The Ribbon Explained

The *Ribbon* is made up of tabs: **File**, **Home**, **Insert** and so on, each of which, when clicked or touched, shows commands that are organized into groups (Figure 8-2). As you make the window bigger, more commands appear on the Ribbon, so to see all of the Ribbon commands you can, maximize the window to make it full screen. The maximize button is a small square in the top right of the window, next to the close button.

Figure 8-2. The Ribbon interface

Each version of an Office program has the same four tabs on the left side of the Ribbon:

- **File** is where you will find the new document and open and save commands.
- **Home** is where all of the text and other formatting commands can be found.
- **Insert** is where you have options to insert images and other items such as sound and video into documents.
- **Page Layout** is where you can control the size and other aspects of your document.

In Microsoft Word, you will also see a **Mailings** tab where you can control mail merges, which can be very useful for small businesses, organizations, and groups to send letters and emails to many people.

In Microsoft Excel, you will see a **Formulas** tab, where you can add automatic calculations to your spreadsheets.

Being Productive with Office

Some features in Microsoft Office can help you be very productive. In the very top left of the window, you will see the *Quick Access Toolbar*. Here are icons you can click/touch for some of the most common tasks (Figure 8-3). By default, there are icons for *Save*, *Undo*, and *Refresh*.

Figure 8-3. Tabs on the Ribbon

If you click/touch the down arrow to the right of these icons, you can add and remove icons from the menu by simply selecting them from the drop-down options menu that appears.

In the top right of the window, just below the minimize, maximize, and close buttons, you will see a small arrow (Figure 8-4). Clicking the arrow will minimize (or maximize) the buttons on the Ribbon so that it only appears when you click/touch on a Ribbon tab. Otherwise, it appears all the time. This can be useful if you have a small screen. There is also a Question Mark icon in the top right of the window that, when clicked, will display help.

Figure 8-4. Hiding the Ribbon and Help

In the bottom right of the window are controls for moving about within pages and viewing your document in different ways, but most importantly, the zoom control (Figure 8-5). You can use this to make your document larger or smaller in the window, which is useful if you find small text difficult to read or if you need to see more of the document on your screen.

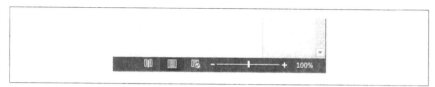

Figure 8-5. Making things bigger or smaller

Using the Desktop in Windows 8

In Chapter 4, I showed you how to snap two desktop windows side by side. There is so much more you can do on the desktop, however.

For instance, if you don't want to keep switching back and forth between the Start screen and desktop when launching programs, you can *pin* programs directly onto the desktop Taskbar, the bar that runs along the bottom of the screen so that they are there all the time, enabling you to get quick access to them.

To do this, right-click on a program (or tap and pull downwards with your finger) and from the App Bar click/touch *Pin to Taskbar*.

Program icons on the Taskbar also have their own *Jumplists*. You can access these by touching the icon and pushing upward or *right-clicking* with your mouse. Each Jumplist contains controls for things you can do with that program, such as launching another instance of it or closing it.

Jumplists also contain a list of recently opened files. You can *pin* a file to the Jumplist so that it always appears there (Figure 8-6). This can be very useful if you have files that you need to access regularly. You can unpin files the same way.

You can also see thumbnail images of open programs, even if they are minimized from the Taskbar. This can be useful if you have many windows open on your desktop or are perhaps using a web browser with many tabs open at the same time. To do this, hover your mouse over an open program on the Taskbar and a thumbnail image of the program will appear (Figure 8-7).

 Please note that you can't do this with a touch gesture.

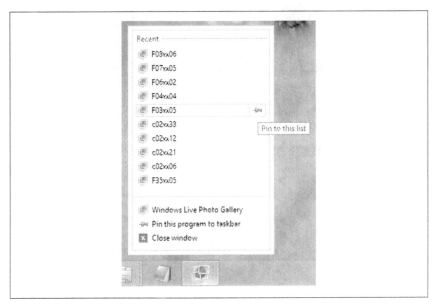

Figure 8-6. Pinning documents to Jumplists

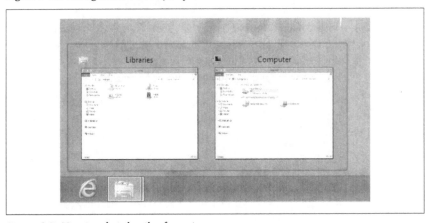

Figure 8-7. Viewing thumbnails of running programs

If you have a lot of windows open, moving your mouse over a thumbnail will temporarily hide all other windows and show you the one you have selected (even if it is minimized itself). You can then, if you want to, switch directly to that window by clicking the thumbnail.

Hiding and Restoring All the Open Desktop Windows

If you have a lot of windows open on your screen and you want to minimize them all, perhaps when you go for a break, you can click/touch with your mouse in the far right of the desktop Taskbar, to the right of the time and date. This will minimize all windows. You can then restore them all by clicking this area again. Moving your mouse cursor to the very bottom right of your screen will temporarily minimize every window. They will be restored when you move your mouse away from this area.

Connecting and Using Projectors and Second Screens

Windows 8 is excellent at detecting additional hardware, such as projectors and secondary displays. You can access these by opening the Charms Menu and clicking *Devices*.

Here you will see a list of additional displays connected to your computer. This includes projectors. Clicking on a display will bring up several options for that display (Figure 8-8).

- **PC Screen Only** will turn off the image to the secondary display.
- **Duplicate** will put the same image on both displays.
- **Extend** will use the second screen to extend your desktop.
- **Second Screen Only** will use only the second display until you unplug it.

Maximizing Battery Life on Your Laptop or Tablet

Battery life is always an important issue for computers. If you have a new Windows 8 tablet, you may be getting 10 hours or more out of your battery, but on a laptop or Windows 8 Pro tablet, you'll more likely be getting just 4 or 5 hours.

You can maximize your battery life by using tools in the *Windows Mobility Center*, which I will talk about in the next section, but other things you can do include:

- Turn off any keyboard backlight.
- Turn down your screen brightness.
- Don't leave programs and apps that will read/write to your hard disk running, such as music players

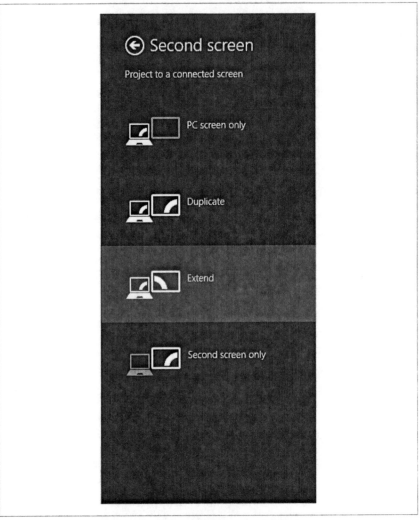

Figure 8-8. Choosing how to extend your display to a second screen

- Turn off WiFi (if your computer has a WiFi on/off switch) and your mobile broadband when you're not using it. You can also do this by switching on Airplane mode. See Chapter 2 for how to do this.

The Windows Mobility Center

The Windows Mobility Center (Figure 8-9) can be found by searching for **Mobility** at the Start screen (it will be in the *Settings* search results). It is the best place to go to balance your battery life with on-the-road performance.

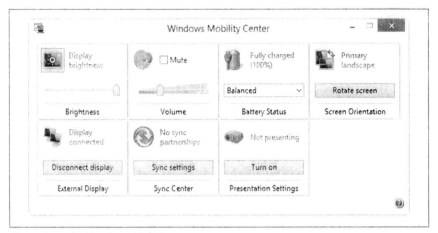

Figure 8-9. The Windows Mobility Center

Here you can adjust your display brightness, speaker volume, and more. Some of the more interesting and useful features are:

- **Battery Status** enables you to choose several different battery modes for your computer, including a power saving mode.
- **Presentation Settings**, if turned on while using your computer to give a presentation, will silence all desktop and other alerts. This includes pop-up messages informing you of new email. Windows will also be prevented from turning off the display during a period of inactivity or going to sleep with this mode activated.

Summary

Windows 8 contains some excellent tools and utilities for being productive and working for long periods away from a power socket. The inclusion of trimmed down versions of Microsoft Office, which is suitable for most everyday tasks, is a welcome bonus, and the Windows Mobility Center is a great way to manage your battery life.

These features, coupled with some of the excellent and sometimes hidden ways you can interact with and use programs on the desktop, make Windows 8 a great tool for being productive, whatever you need it for and wherever you are.

Sometimes you will want to use older software with Windows 8, perhaps software that you're really comfortable with or that you need for a specific task. In Chapter 9, I will show you how to make sure this software runs properly in Windows 8.

Using Older Software and Programs

Even though there are already a great many new apps specifically for Windows 8, many of which are completely free, you might still have older desktop programs that you like to use or even brand new desktop programs.

There's a *Desktop* tile on the Windows 8 Start screen, but how do you install desktop programs? Do you get it all from the Windows Store, and how can you make sure that the older programs you've come to either love or rely on still work?

 You can only install desktop programs on your tablet if it is running Windows 8 Pro. If you want to use desktop software, you should ask if it runs the Pro version before making your purchase.

Top Tips from This Chapter

1. Not all Windows XP programs will work in Windows 8, but you can turn on *Compatibility Mode* for programs that don't work properly.

2. Do not allow program installations unless you *specifically* intended to install it because it could be malware.

3. You can uninstall apps and programs directly from the Start screen by right-clicking them, or tapping and dragging down.

Windows Tablets and Desktop Programs

If you have a consumer Windows 8 tablet, you will not be able to install desktop programs onto the computer. The desktop still exists, and you will know that you have this type of tablet because you will have feature-limited versions of Microsoft's Office programs Word, Excel, PowerPoint, and OneNote already installed.

The reason you can't install desktop programs on Windows 8 tablets is because of incompatibilities with the different type of hardware your tablet has inside it. Simply put, Windows desktop programs won't run on this hardware because it is incompatible with it. You can still install desktop programs on a Windows 8 Pro tablet, though.

Installing Desktop Programs in Windows 8

So where do you get desktop programs and how do you install them? It is most common to download programs from the Internet, and some desktop programs can be downloaded from the Windows Store, but you can also install programs from a USB flash drive or a CD/DVD.

When you plug a disk, a USB flash drive, or another type of drive into your Windows 8 computer, a pop-up alert will appear in the top right of your screen asking what you want to do with it (Figure 9-1).

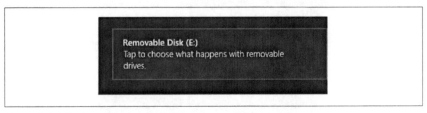

Figure 9-1. Windows alerts you when you insert a disk or drive

You are given several choices in this pop-up alert (Figure 9-2). If you intend to install programs, you will probably see the option to *Run Setup.exe*, which is the usual name for a program installer.

Figure 9-2. Do you want to run setup.exe?

You will also see options to *Open a folder…* to view the contents of the disk. You may want to do this if you are copying files from the disk, or if Windows 8 has not recognized the correct program to install.

If you tell Windows to install the programs, you are taken to the desktop and the program will install from there. You will be presented with a security panel asking you to confirm that you do *actually* want to install this programs. This security feature is here to help prevent viruses and other malware from making changes to your computer.

Be Careful What Programs You Install

While all apps downloaded and installed from the Windows Store have been scanned for malware by Microsoft, programs you install or download from another source do not come with a guarantee that it won't contain a virus.

Try to avoid installing trial programs and/or too many programs. Installing trialware means that you are likely to end up with lots of expired programs that won't run (usually after 30 days), will take up space, and could cause other problems. Installing too many programs could cause your computer to become unstable over time.

Installing a Program in Compatibility Mode

Windows 8 is very good at detecting if programs might not run correctly—for instance, if the program you wish to install was designed and written for an earlier version of Windows, such as XP. If this happens, it will alert you that there might be problems with the program and that it might not run properly (Figure 9-3).

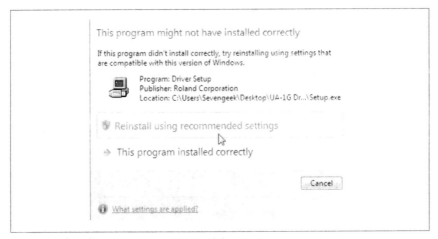

Figure 9-3. Installing programs in Compatibility Mode

If you know the program works fine in Windows 8 (most programs that work in Windows 7 will also work in Windows 8) then click/touch *This program installed correctly*, but if you are not sure, click/touch *Reinstall using recommended settings*. Windows 8 will then reinstall the program, applying different settings that make older programs more likely to run without problems.

Troubleshooting Program Compatibility

If you are still having problems getting programs to run properly, you can set the compatibility for the program manually. Windows 8 provides a wizard to help you through this issue (Figure 9-4). To set the compatibility for a program manually, follow these instructions:

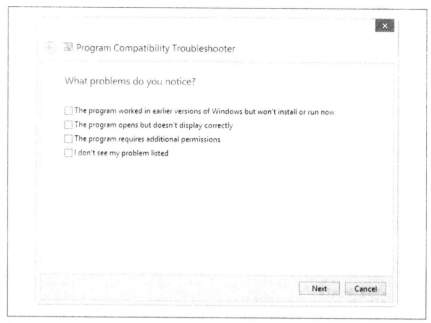

Figure 9-4. Manually troubleshooting program compatibility

1. From the Start screen or All Apps view, *right-click* on the relevant program.
2. From the App Bar, click/touch *Open File Location* and a window will open with the program highlighted.
3. *Right-click* (touch and hold) on the program and an options menu will appear.
4. Select *Troubleshoot Compatibility* and the Automatic Troubleshooter will appear.
5. Click/Touch the *Troubleshoot Program* button.

You are now asked a series of questions about how the program worked in the past. At the end of this process, Windows automatically sets the compatibility for the program and asks you to test it. If it still does not work, it will allow you to change the compatibility settings and try again.

Running Programs on the Windows Desktop

Icons for installed desktop programs appear on your Start screen. In Chapter 4, I showed you how you can arrange and organize Tiles and icons on the Start screen, including hiding them. Some desktop programs will also install utilities (including uninstallers), which you may want to hide to keep the Start screen tidy and easy to use.

You can run a desktop program from the Start screen by clicking/touching it. If it is a desktop program you are starting, you will immediately be taken to the desktop and the program will be started.

Making the Best of the Taskbar

In Chapter 4, I showed you how you can pin desktop programs to the Windows 8 desktop Taskbar. If you spend a lot of time working on the desktop, this is a good way to avoid having to switch between the Start screen and the desktop to run a program.

When a program is running, you can also *right-click* on its desktop icon and select *Pin to Taskbar* (or *Unpin from Taskbar*).

Uninstalling Desktop Programs in Windows 8

Uninstalling programs in Windows 8 is, if anything, slightly easier than in previous versions of Windows. To uninstall a program, *right-click* (or *tap and drag downwards*) its icon on the Start screen or in the All Apps view, and from the App Bar, select *Uninstall*.

Apps will be uninstalled automatically, but if you are uninstalling a program, you will be taken to the *Programs and Features* window on the desktop. Here, you will need to find the program by looking for its name in the list.

Once you have found the program, click/tap on the program name. In the toolbar above the list of programs, you will see an *Uninstall* or a *Remove* option appear. Click/Touch this to uninstall the program (Figure 9-5).

 You can click/touch on the column headers *Name*, *Installed On*, etc., to sort the installed programs in different ways; for example, showing the most recently installed programs at the top of the list.

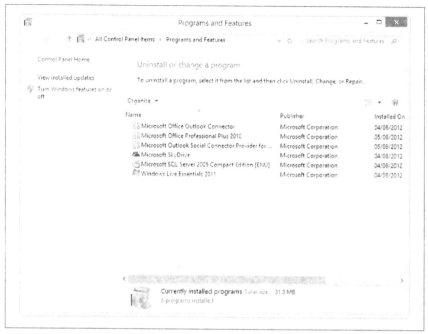

Figure 9-5. Uninstalling a desktop program

Summary

Windows 8 is compatible with most of the programs that ran on Windows 7 and Windows Vista. Sadly, it is not compatible with all Windows XP programs. You might find that just small parts of an older program fail to work. I have an old program I like to use that does this and I can get by with it in Windows 8 because the bit that doesn't work is a feature I don't really need.

The compatibility settings can go some way to helping make older programs run in Windows 8 but if, in the case of the program I like to use, it calls a Windows feature that's long since been removed, there's nothing that can be done to make it work properly.

I've spoken throughout this book and in this chapter about the dangers of having malware on your computer. In Chapter 10, I'll show you how to keep your family safe when using your computer and going online.

Keeping You and Your Family Safe

One of the biggest challenges people face when using computers is keeping safe when they're on the Internet. How do you keep malware off your computer, how can you tell a fake website from a real one, and how do you keep your children safe from inappropriate web content and unsuitable games?

These are concerns, not just for parents but also for every Internet user. In this chapter, I want to show you how Windows 8 can help keep you, your friends, and your family safe.

Top Tips from This Chapter

1. Each user should her their own account to separate her personal files and Internet favorites.
2. Criminals will try and trick you into installing malware/viruses; do not click/touch things casually.
3. The Family Safety features in Windows 8 can help keep your children safe online.

Setting Up Additional Users on Your Computer

When you first use Windows 8, you will be asked to create a user account, either a local one on the computer or one created using a Microsoft account. This will have the same login you use for a Hotmail or Live email account or for your Xbox.

When you are using Windows 8 in a family environment, it's always a good idea to give each user his own user account, but what is the difference between a local account and a Microsoft Account?

- A local account is stored only on a single computer, and it's exclusive to that computer. It only gives a person access to that one computer. It doesn't come with an email address, nor does it come with the ability to purchase apps or games.

- A Microsoft account synchronizes your computer with your email, calendar, and contacts, and also allows you to buy apps and games from the Store. This account type also allows you to log into multiple Windows 8 computers and automatically see all of *your* own Internet favorites, email, and apps on each and every computer.

This doesn't mean that anybody with a Hotmail or Xbox Live account can simply gain access to your computer. You need to specifically give them their own account first, and I will show you how to do this shortly.

The other benefit to people having their own user accounts is that it keeps each person's files and Internet favorites separate, so they don't get mixed up and one person's files can't be deleted by another person accidentally.

To create a new user account, you need to go to the *PC Settings* panel. Remember, you get to this by opening the Charms menu, clicking/touching Settings, then clicking/touching Change PC Settings.

1. Click/Touch *Users* in the left-hand panel (Figure 10-1).

2. Click/Touch *Add a user* in the main panel.

   a. To add someone who already has a Microsoft Account, enter her email address. You will need to be connected to the Internet at this point.

   b. To sign up for a Microsoft Account, click/touch *Sign up for a new email address*. You will need to be connected to the Internet to create an account.

   c. To create a local user account, click/touch *Don't want this user to sign in with a Microsoft Account?* This does not require Internet access.

You will be asked for a password. This is required with a Microsoft Account but it is optional for a local account. For example, you might not want to set a password for young children because it is easy for them to forget, and do they need their own password on your computer anyway?

 When starting your computer, if you do not see the user account you want displayed, click/touch the back button next to the user picture to display all the user accounts on the computer you can log in with.

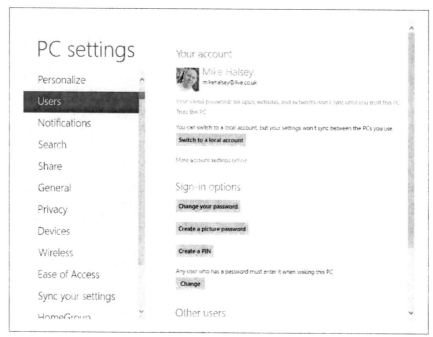

Figure 10-1. The Users panel in PC Settings.bmp

Viruses, Malware, and Phishing Explained

So you've created your user accounts and you're browsing the Internet. Are you safe doing this? Well, there are criminals who want to trick you into installing viruses onto your computer and surrendering personal and sensitive information.

I'm going to lump all nasties and meanies together under the *malware* name but technically, malware is a malicious program, file, and email intended to steal your personal information (credit card details, passwords, date of birth, mother's maiden name) or to trick you into revealing them yourself.

Malware spreads in several ways:

- Websites that try to trick you into downloading a file pretending that you need it to play video or perform a specific action.

- Downloaded files from file-sharing websites; these are commonly laden with malware.

- Infected email attachments, Adobe PDF files, or Word, Excel, or Power-Point documents are common targets.
- Infected storage devices such as USB flash drives.

The simple rule is that if you did not visit a website to download something, DON'T download anything. If you go to YouTube and receive a message saying a *codec* is required to watch a video, it's lying. If you go to any other website that tries to download files to your computer, just say *No*.

If you are ever in doubt about attachments sent by a friend or colleague, just email them asking if they intended to send it, before you open it.

Phishing is the act of sending emails that try to trick you into believing that they're from a reputable bank or website (such as PayPal). They say they need you to log in to confirm your security or personal details. The link they provide will always take you to a fake website and your details will be stolen.

The rule here is that NO reputable bank or website will EVER email you asking you to log in to confirm your security details.

Fake Antivirus Software: Be Alert

One other thing to be aware of is when a website says they have scanned your computer and found malware, but their software can get rid of it for you. NO website is capable of scanning your computer for malware without your express permission. These websites are *always* fake and their software is malware intended to scam you out of your credit card and other personal details.

Using Windows Defender to Keep Your Computer Safe

The good news is that all versions of Windows 8 come with antimalware software built in. It's call Windows Defender and you can find it by searching for *defender* at the Start screen. You probably won't need to open it, though, because it will update itself and scan regularly in the background.

Windows Defender is updated through Windows Update, so it is very important not to turn that off! I will show you how to use Windows Update in Chapter 11.

If you do want to open Windows Defender, it has a very friendly interface that changes color from green to amber and red to alert you to its current status (Figure 10-2). If it is not currently up to date, an *Update* button will appear on the front screen and you can choose to run either a *Quick Scan*, which scans Windows and your documents, or a *Full Scan*, which scans every file on your computer for malware.

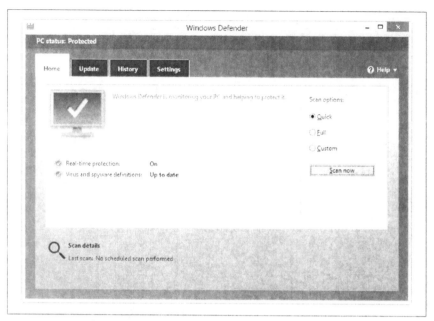

Figure 10-2. Windows Defender

Browsing Safely with Internet Explorer 10

Internet Explorer is very good at alerting you to both safe and unsafe websites when you visit them, and also to malware and malicious downloads. The first thing it does is highlight the actual name of the website. In Figure 10-3, you can see that the name *paypal.com* is bolder than the rest of the text. This is so you can tell if you are at the correct website, perhaps because you've clicked on a link in an email.

Figure 10-3. Internet Explorer tells you when websites are safe or not

Whenever you visit a website for banking or shopping, you will also see a padlock symbol on the right of the address bar on any page that requires you to type personal details. This sometimes also appears with the name of the company and this is assurance that a valid security certificate is owned by this company, and that all your personal details are encrypted before your web browser sends them on.

You will also see in Figure 10-3 that the address bar has turned green. This is Internet Explorer's way of telling you that this website is known to be safe. If the address bar turns red, then you are visiting a website that is known to be insecure and may contain malware. You should leave the website immediately.

Internet Explorer also scans all the documents and files you download. It does this using Windows Defender and a feature in Internet Explorer called *SmartScreen*. This checks all downloads against lists of known safe and unsafe files. If it thinks a file might be potentially dangerous to you or your computer, it will alert you and ask you if you want to continue.

Setting Up and Using Family Safety

When you set up a user account, Windows 8 will ask you if this account is for a child. If it is, Windows can give you reports showing what that user has done online, but this doesn't stop them from visiting inappropriate websites or viewing unsuitable content to begin with. That is where the Windows 8 Family Safety features come in.

If you have young children, you will want to keep them safe online. Windows 8 contains an excellent and fully featured set of Family Safety options in which you can choose:

- What times of day and on what days they can use the computer
- What types of games they can play
- What websites they can visit

You can open the Family Safety area by searching for *family* at the Start screen. You will find it under the *Settings* search results.

 To use Family Safety, your child must already have his own user account created in PC Settings and your own user account *must* have a password on it. This prevents the child from changing the parental control settings himself.

Always use strong passwords. It is preferable to use a password that is ten characters or more in length and contains a mixture of upper- and lowercase letters, as well as numbers and symbols. (Remember, you can substitute some numbers and symbols for letters, e.g., 1 = i or l, & = a, 5 = s or S.) I will show you more ways to create a strong password in Chapter 12.

At the main Family Safety panel, click/touch on the child's account for which you want to create controls. You need to set up each child's account individually.

You will see a button to turn the Family Safety on or off for this child (see Figure 10-4). You can also turn activity reporting for the child on and off. These activity reports are available at any time by clicking the *View activity reports* link on the right side of the page.

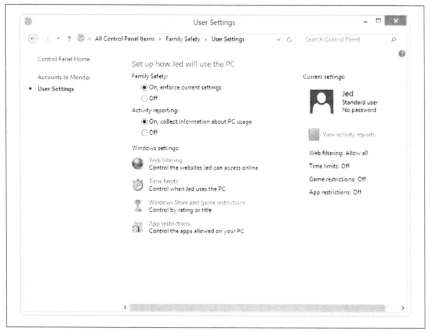

Figure 10-4. Setting Family Safety

There are four main categories of Family Safety controls you can set. The allowed programs category is quite complex and you will probably not want to use it, but the other categories are excellent and include the following.

Windows Web Filter

Here, you can block certain types of websites on the account based on five easy-to-understand *filtering levels*:

- **Allow list only**, where you manually specify the website that can be visited, although this can be time consuming
- **Child-friendly**, in which all adult websites and content are blocked

- **General interest** expands the list of child-friendly websites for slightly older children of school age
- **Online communication** allows children to access email and social networking websites
- **Warn an adult** will provide unlimited access but will warn the child when she might be visiting an adult website

You can also click/touch the link *Allow or Block Websites* in the lefthand panel to customize the list of websites that children can and cannot visit. This is useful if a website is automatically blocked when you want to allow it or when a child might it need for school (Figure 10-5).

Figure 10-5. Allowing or blocking specific websites

Time Limits

This is where you can control the time of day and days of the week that the child can use the computer, or just the maximum number of hours that the computer can be used each day (Figure 10-6). You can specify when the child can use the computer in the *Set curfew* controls by coloring in a chart. You can drag your finger or mouse around this chart to specify the blocks of time when the computer cannot be used.

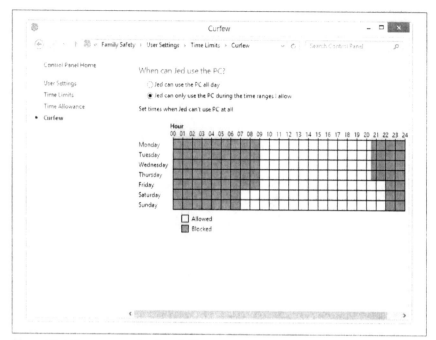

Figure 10-6. You can specify when children can use a computer

The computer is not automatically shut down out of these times; the child is given plenty of warning by Windows 8 that he or she is coming to the end of the allocated time and that, perhaps, it is time for bed.

Games

Here, you can block certain games according to their rating so that only games that are rated as suitable for your child's age can be played. Note, however, that not all games are rated this way and so some games might slip past this certification (Figure 10-7). This does also not block Internet games that are played online and not directly installed on your computer.

Summary

It's fairly straightforward to stay safe with Windows 8, because it not only comes with all the basic security a family needs, but out of the box, it's also set up the way you need it.

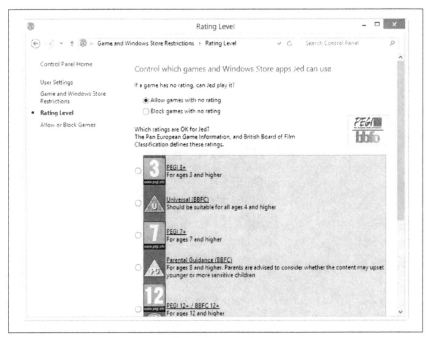

Figure 10-7. You can block unsuitable games in Family Safety

The Family Safety options in Windows 8 is an excellent way to keep your children safe online, and the lists of safe and unsafe websites that Windows 8 uses to determine which websites are suitable for your children to visit are being constantly monitored by Microsoft and security organizations. The ability to add or block specific websites from this list manually is an additional added bonus.

As is always the advice, it's best to take an interest in what your children do online so that you can monitor them and make sure that they're safe and not exposed to unsuitable material.

Now that you and your family are safe, in Chapter 11, I'll show you how you can keep your copy of Windows 8 running safely and smoothly so that it doesn't cause you problems.

Keeping Your Computer Running Smoothly

One of the biggest concerns facing home computer users is the thought that sooner or later something's going to go wrong, and either the computer won't start, or it will misbehave. This can result in being without your computer for a while and paying expensive repair costs.

As the author of *Troubleshoot and Optimize Windows 8 Inside Out*, I'd like to share with you some of the *best* ways that you can keep Windows 8 running smoothly and can rescue it easily in the event that something goes wrong.

Top Tips from This Chapter

1. Always keep a regular and up-to-date backup copy of your files!
2. You can *Refresh* Windows 8 easily to a working copy if it starts to malfunction.
3. You can create a *Recovery Drive* that can be used to rescue Windows 8 in the event that it won't start.

How to Keep Your Files Backed Up

Files and documents on your computer may be important, so if something disastrous happens to your computer or if you have to reinstall Windows from scratch, you'll be pretty upset if they are wiped. This is why the *most* important thing you can ever do with a computer is to keep regular backups of your files.

Windows 8 includes an excellent backup program that you can find by searching for *recovery* at the Start screen and running *Windows 7 File Recovery* from the *Settings* results. It can be set to automatically keep an updated copy of your files backed up, and is very easy to use (Figure 11-1).

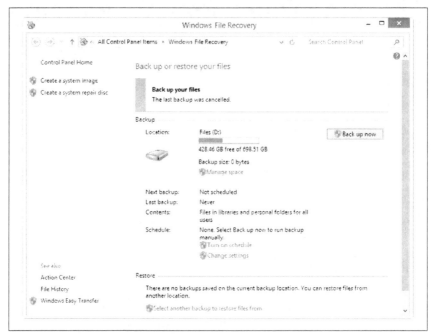

Figure 11-1. Windows 7 File Recovery Panel

 The best place to keep a backup copy of your files is on an external hard disk. These are very cheap and can often be plugged in to your Internet router, which allows the files to be accessed by any computer in your home.

1. At the Windows 7 File Recovery panel, click/touch the *Set up backup* link on the right-hand side.

2. You will then be asked where you want to store your backups (Figure 11-2).

   a. If you are using a network location, such as an external hard disk plugged into your Internet router, then click/touch the *Save on a Network* button. This brings up a new window where you can click/touch the *Browse* button to find your hard disk on the network.

3. Once you have found the correct hard disk, click/touch the *OK* button.

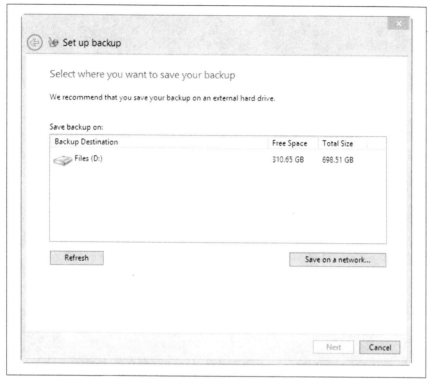

Figure 11-2. Choosing a backup location

When you have selected your backup location, click/touch *Next* and then you will have two backup choices (Figure 11-3).

- *Let Windows choose* what to back up. This will back up your documents, pictures, music, and video libraries, along with other things, such as your Internet favorites. It will also back up Windows 8 itself, complete with all the software you have installed.

- *Let me choose* what to back up gives you complete control over what is backed up on your computer.

So what's the difference between these two options? Well, you might only have a small hard disk to back up your files to, and a full backup of Windows 8 and all your software can take up a lot of space. You might also have a second hard disk in your computer containing additional files, perhaps work files that you want to include in the backup. For both of these circumstances, the *Let me choose* option is best.

Figure 11-3. The Backup Wizard

If you choose this second option, then after pressing the *Next* button, you will be asked what you want to include in your backup (Figure 11-4). This is presented as a list that can be expanded by clicking the arrows to the left of each item. You can select (and deselect) items for the backup by checking and unchecking the boxes. Click/Touch the *Next* button when you are happy with your choices.

At the very bottom of this list, there is an option to *Include a system image* of Windows. This is the option of creating a full backup copy of Windows 8. It is extremely useful because if Windows won't start, you can restore it and be up and running again quickly with all your files, documents, and programs safe and intact. If you are short on space, you can create one separately on a different hard disk or on DVDs, and I will show you how to do this later in this chapter. Uncheck this box if you do not want to create a backup copy of Windows at this time.

Finally, you will be presented with a screen that shows you what you have chosen to back up, where it is going to be backed up, and how often. It is here

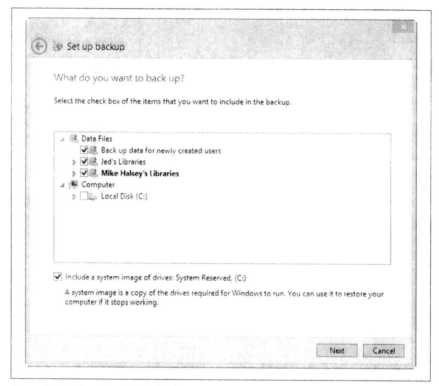

Figure 11-4. *Choosing what to back up*

that you can click/touch the *Change schedule* link to specify when and how often backups should be kept (Figure 11-5).

 I would recommend that you keep backups at least once a month, but if you make regular changes to documents and add new files, you should back them up every week.

When you are ready to start your first backup, click/touch the *Save settings and backup* button to begin your backup for the first time.

Restoring Your Files from a Backup

Once you have created your first file backup, the Windows 7 File Recovery page will display details of when the last backup was completed and what was backed up. Here, you will see a link that you can click/touch to restore your

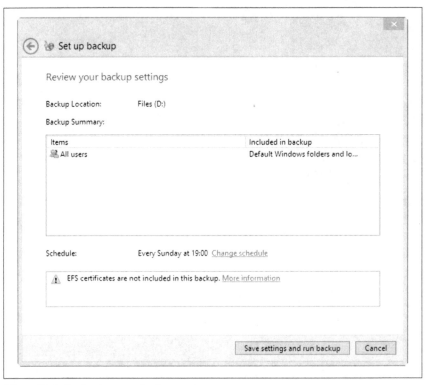

Figure 11-5. Reviewing your backup settings

files. You don't need to restore all of them if they've not all been lost, however, and the wizard will guide you through what files you want restored from the backup.

Restoring Windows 8 from a Backup

There are two ways to restore Windows 8. If you have used the Windows 7 File Recovery panel to create a backup copy of Windows 8 itself, then you'll want to restore this in the event of a disaster.

If you need to restore your copy of Windows 8, this usually means that Windows 8 won't start and the *Startup Repair* feature will appear when you turn on your computer. You will be prompted to try and repair the computer, but if Startup Repair can't fix your computer, you will be presented with several options. The one you want is *System Image Recovery* (Figure 11-6).

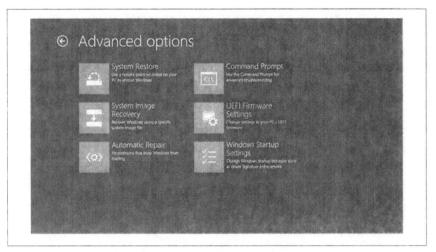

Figure 11-6. Restoring a backup Windows image

 If you use WiFi to connect your computer to your Internet router and your backup copy of Windows is on the network, perhaps on a USB hard disk plugged into the router, you will need to physically connect your computer to the router to restore Windows from the backup. Ask at your local computer store for a *Network cable*. You might need 5 or 10 feet or more of cable to stretch between the computer and the router.

System Image Recovery will automatically select your backup image of Windows 8 if you are physically connected to the hard disk containing your backup as per the previous tip. The restore can be started with a couple of clicks, and Windows 8 can be restored to working condition in less than 20 minutes on average.

Restoring Windows 8 from a backup image will also require you to restore your files from a backup because these files might be wiped during the reinstallation process. You can easily restore your files from a backup using the instructions I detailed earlier in this chapter.

 You can manually create a backup image of Windows 8 too (again, from the Windows 7 File Recovery panel) by clicking the *Create a system image* link on the left side of the panel.

Refreshing Windows 8

The System Image backup can be complicated for some people, however, and there is a better and easier option available. This is especially useful if you don't use desktop software and stick to using apps. This feature is called *Refresh*.

1. Open the Charms menu.
2. Click/Touch *Settings*.
3. Click/Touch *Change PC Settings*.
4. In the *General* section of PC Settings in the *Refresh your PC without affecting your files* section, click/touch the *Get started* button (Figure 11-7).

Figure 11-7. Starting Refresh

At the next screen, Windows 8 will tell you what it will do (Figure 11-8). Refreshing your computer *won't* delete any of your files but you will need to reinstall your apps from the Windows Store (the Store will tell you which apps you have already purchased to make this easier). You will also need to reinstall any desktop software you have been using. The important thing, however, is that your files will be safe so long as they are stored in the main libraries and you haven't stored any somewhere else!

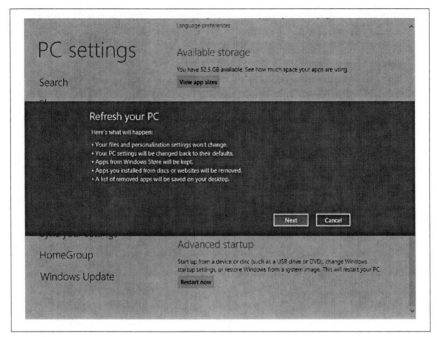

Figure 11-8. Refreshing your copy of Windows 8

When you are ready to start the *Refresh* process, click/touch the *Next* button.

Creating a Recovery Drive

If your computer won't start at all, you can still restore it from a backup or Refresh it. To do this, you first need to create a *Recovery Drive*. This is a USB Flash Drive that you can use to start your computer.

To create a Recovery Drive, search for *recovery* at the Start screen and run *Recovery* from the *Settings* search results. In the panel that appears, click/touch the *Create a recovery drive* link (Figure 11-9).

You will need to have a USB flash drive plugged into your computer, one that you're not using for anything else. If it is a large enough flash drive, and if your computer came with a Recovery Partition when you bought it, you can also copy across this backup copy of Windows 8 to the drive. This means that if Windows 8 won't start and you can't restore it from a backup image or a Refresh image, you can still restore it to how it was when you bought the computer.

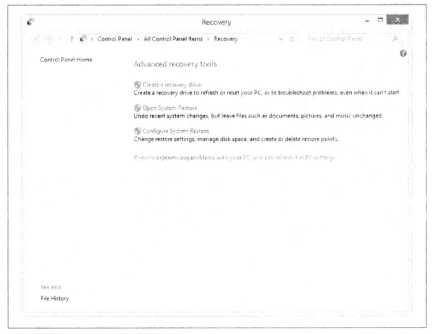

Figure 11-9. Creating a recovery drive

 When purchasing a USB Flash Drive large enough to store the system backup copy of Windows that came with your computer, choose one that is 32GB or preferably 64GB in size.

Using System Restore to Rescue Windows

In the *Recovery* panel, you will also find *System Restore*. A restore point is a snapshot of critical Windows files taken when a change is made, such as installing a new piece of hardware, installing new software, or running Windows Update.

Should something go wrong and Windows become unstable, you can click/touch *Open System Restore* to find a restore point that was made recently and when your computer was running well. By clicking/touching a restore point and then clicking/touching the *Next* button, you can restore Windows files to this point. This does not affect your files and documents.

Maintaining Windows 8

So far, this chapter has focused on backing up and restoring Windows and your files, should disaster strike. But ideally, you just want to keep Windows 8 running smoothly so that problems don't occur, right?

Well, Windows 8 is able to perform maintenance tasks on itself. You can access this feature by searching for *maintenance* at the Start screen and clicking *Change automatic maintenance settings* in the *Settings* search results.

In the window that appears, you have just two options (Figure 11-10). When does automatic maintenance run and can the computer be woken up to run it? This second option will only work if the computer is set to Sleep rather than shut down, and if it is plugged in. If this is unlikely, then try setting maintenance to run at a time when you will often be using the computer, such as in the evening. Maintenance won't prevent the computer from working and it won't stop you from doing what you are doing.

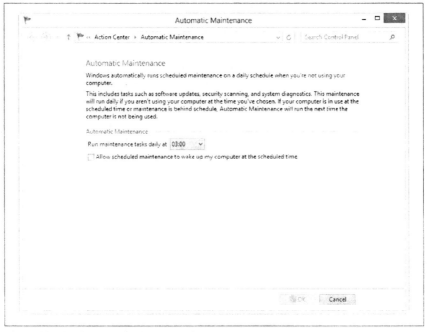

Figure 11-10. Changing the Automatic Maintenance Settings

The maintenance tool will clean up unwanted temporary files that accrue during daily use of your computer, perform diagnostic tests, and make sure your security and Windows Updates are up to date. This really is a great solution because it takes all of the hassle out of keeping your Windows 8 computer running smoothly.

You can always check the *Windows Update* settings manually in PC Settings, and indeed I would recommend you do this now and again, but the automatic maintenance of Windows 8 should provide all the peace of mind that you need.

Summary

Windows 8 is great at maintaining itself, but in the event that something *does* go wrong, all is not lost. If you only or predominantly use Windows 8 apps and not desktop software, the *Refresh* option is a great way to get Windows working again when it misbehaves. Sometimes, though—for example, after you've just installed a Windows update—you will know that the PC is misbehaving. In this case, a simple System Restore will commonly fix the problem.

If disaster strikes, then you're still not out of options. It's wise to create a *Recovery Drive* and a System Image copy of Windows 8 if you have enough spare hard disk space for one, either on an external USB hard disk or on a second internal hard disk in your computer.

You should *always* make sure you keep regular and up-to-date backups of your files. This is by far the most important thing you can do on your computer. If you can also try to keep a copy of your files outside of your home, perhaps in an Internet service such as Microsoft's SkyDrive, it will help protect your files should the worst happen and you suffer a theft or a fire.

There have been a lot of tips in this chapter for keeping Windows 8 running smoothly, and in Chapter 12, I'm going to share with you even more top tips for getting the maximum benefit out of Windows 8.

More Top Tips for Using Windows 8

Throughout this book, I've shown you how to do the things that you'll most commonly want to do with your Windows 8 computer. But what about all the other cool stuff that makes using your desktop PC, laptop, or tablet *really* easy? In this chapter, I'll share with you my favorite tips and tricks for getting Windows 8 to work for you, and for making your Windows 8 computer a really fun thing to use.

Use a Picture Password

Windows 8 practically begs you to log into your computer using a Microsoft Account. This does have some big advantages, such as automatically setting up your email, calendar, Internet favorites, and the Windows Stores for apps, music, and videos. To keep yourself secure, though, you will need a strong password, and I'll show you how to create one in the next section of this chapter.

Typing this long password into Windows 8 every time you want to use the computer can be annoying, so why not create a picture password instead? You can choose any picture on your computer and use it to unlock your computer by touching and tapping it. The actions you can choose from include tapping the picture, drawing straight lines on it, and drawing circles.

Picture passwords can be every bit as secure as a regular strong password because they can seem completely random. In Figure 12-1, you will see a picture of baby Gilbert and you might tickle his tummy, poke his nose, and then draw a circle around his face to unlock your computer.

Figure 12-1. Creating a picture password

Use a Secure Password

Picture passwords aside, I would always advise that you use strong passwords for everything else, such as your email, websites you visit, banking, and so on. Here are my top tips for creating a really secure password.

A really secure password should be at least 12 characters in length. Consider the following tips as well:

- Use a mixture of upper and lower case characters, numbers, and symbols.
- Substitute some numbers and symbols for letters. (e.g., 5 or $ instead of s or S, 1 or [instead of i or L and () instead of 0).
- Use a code you'll remember, such as capitalizing the second or third letter of each word.
- String words together to make a strong core password that you can use for everything.

- Mix into your core password, perhaps at the beginning or the end, the first few letters of the website or service you are logging into to make that password unique to that service.
- Check how secure your password is at *http://www.howsecureismypass word.net.*

Get Extra Information from the Start Screen

The Live Tiles on Start Screen Apps are a great way to get lots of information about a very wide range of subjects, all really quickly and at a glance. You might not find a general use for a Finance App, for example, although its Live Tile might also be able to give you helpful information about currency exchange rates.

 You can search within an app by opening, for example, *Search* from the Charms menu to search for new games or other software in the Windows Store.

Make Sure You Keep Regular Backups

Your files, pictures, music, and videos are the most precious things you will *ever* keep on your computer, and it's essential to keep them securely and properly backed up. I showed you how to create backups in Chapter 11, but there are other tips I can offer.

I would always recommend that you keep two backups, one locally on an external USB hard disk (and these are very cheap these days) and another using a cloud backup service such as Microsoft SkyDrive, Amazon S3, Mozy, or DropBox.

You should always keep regular backups; once a month is usually best but you might want to keep them more regularly if you use your computer for college or work, or if you add or change files often.

If you can't use an Internet cloud backup service, perhaps you can keep a copy of your backup off site on a USB hard disk that you bring home once a month to update. Perhaps you have a USB hard disk you can leave with a friend or family member. This helps protect your files from fire, flood, and theft.

Don't rely on CDs and DVDs for backups. These can degrade over time, making them unreadable, and there's never any clue as to when they will fail.

 If you *really* miss the Start Menu from earlier versions of Windows, there are several ways either to restore it or get an alternative. The best place to start is *http://www.stardock.com*, which provides a wide range of Windows customization products. Another option is ViStart, which you can download from *http://www.lee-soft.com/vistart*.

Create a Custom Refresh Image

In Chapter 11, I showed you how to refresh your computer if it malfunctions. While this will restore Windows 8 to a fully working copy, you will have to reinstall all of your desktop software and apps afterwards.

You can create a custom refresh image, however, but for this you will need a second hard disk or a rescue partition in your computer with enough free space on it.

A custom refresh image differs from the standard one included with Windows 8 in that it will include your user accounts and Windows settings. This can make getting up and running again after refreshing your computer much quicker and simpler, especially if you have changed time-consuming settings, such as Family Safety.

You can check if you have this by opening *File Explorer* on the desktop and clicking on *Computer* in the left panel. If you see a **D:** hard disk listed, you have a second hard disk in your computer.

To create a custom refresh image, press the *Windows Key+X* on your keyboard. In the menu that opens, click/touch *Command Prompt (Admin)* (Figure 12-2). You will also need to click/touch *okay* on a security prompt.

In the window that appears, type the following two commands, pressing the Enter key on your keyboard after each one:

mkdir D:\Win8Refresh
    This creates a new store folder for your custom Refresh image.

recimg -CreateImage D:\Win8Refresh
    This creates a custom Refresh image for your copy of Windows 8.

Programs and Features
Mobility Center
Power Options
Event Viewer
System
Device Manager
Disk Management
Computer Management
Command Prompt
Command Prompt (Admin)

Task Manager
Control Panel
File Explorer
Search
Run

Desktop

Figure 12-2. Opening the Command Prompt

When you buy a new PC, you should always keep all the disks and manuals that came with it safe and together in a dry place. A shoebox is usually a great storage box for these and you should add any extra disks and documentation that you get with new hardware and software to this box when you buy new things for your computer. If you need to reinstall Windows 8 or if you want to upgrade your computer, you will often need these disks and manuals.

Using the Calendar and Clocks on the Desktop Taskbar

If you use your computer for work and use the desktop a lot of the time, there are powerful calendar tools you can access and you can set clocks for different time zones from your Taskbar.

To access the time and date functions in Windows 8, click/touch on the time and date on the far right side of the Taskbar, and a date and time panel will open. Here's how you control it.

You can control the date panel by clicking the small left and right arrows above the calendar (Figure 12-3). These will move the calendar backwards or forwards a month. You can also click/touch on the month and year between the arrows to switch to different calendar views. This allows you to quickly move to different months and years.

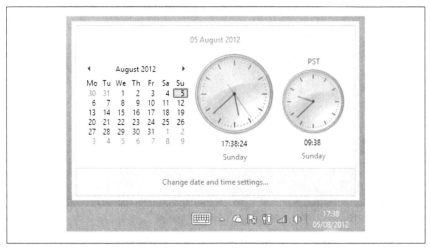

Figure 12-3. The Date and Time Panel

You can add additional clocks for different time zones to this panel by clicking the *Change date and time settings* link at the bottom of the panel. In the window that appears, click/touch the *Additional clocks* tab and you can add up to two more clocks, specifying the time zone you want for each one.

Choosing the Programs that Open Files

If you find that a file is opening with the wrong program or isn't opening at all, you can fix this by searching for *default* at the Start screen and click/touch *Default Programs* when it appears in the search results. In the next panel, you have several options, including choosing what happens when you plug things in, such as USB flash drives, CDs, DVDs, and external hard disks to your computer (Figure 12-4).

To change the program or app a file opens with, click/touch the *Set your default programs* link. This will open a new panel where, on the left, you will see a list of all your installed software and apps. Find the program that you want to use as the default to open this particular type of file. For example, if you want to open music files in Windows Media Player, find *Windows Media Player* in the list and click/touch it.

In the right side of the panel, you can choose to set this program as the default for every type of file it can open, which in this case is music and video, or you can *Choose defaults for this program* instead, if perhaps you want to use it for music but not videos (Figure 12-5).

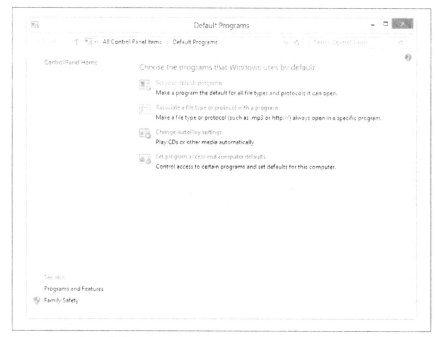

Figure 12-4. The Default Programs Panel

Managing Your Default Sound Devices

If you find that sound on your computer isn't working correctly—for example, if you've plugged in headphones but the sound is still coming out of your speakers—it's easy to change the default sound device. To do this, go to the desktop and *right-click* with your mouse on the speaker icon next to the time and date on the Taskbar (Figure 12-6).

From the options that appear, click/touch *Playback devices* and this will open a new panel showing all the sound playback devices in or attached to your computer. To change the default sound device, click/touch the device you want to use for sound and then click/touch the *Set Default* button at the bottom of the panel (Figure 12-7).

 When you have finished, you may need to set the default playback device back to what it was originally so that you can continue to listen to sound and music (e.g., if you switched temporarily from speakers to headphones).

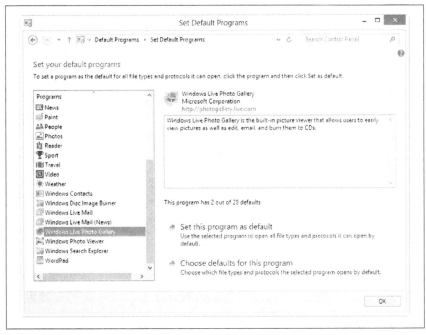

Figure 12-5. Setting the default program

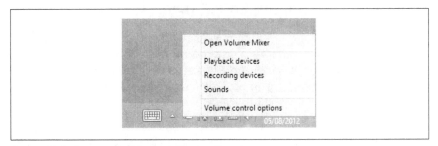

Figure 12-6. Opening the Playback Devices Panel

Turn It Off and On Again

This is the perennial troubleshooting tip and the most commonly given piece of advice by computer professionals. If you find that something isn't working or is malfunctioning, just try turning everything off and then on again. You'd be surprised how many times this fixes a problem.

If you still have trouble, Windows 8 comes with some easy-to-use automated troubleshooters (Figure 12-8). To find these, search for *troubleshooting* at the Start screen and run *Troubleshooting* from the *Settings* search results.

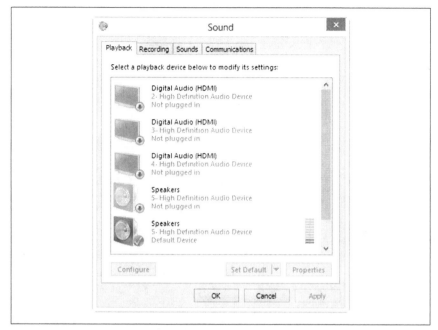

Figure 12-7. Setting the default sound device

 Opening *Settings* from the Charms menu inside an app can reveal additional options for that app that will appear in the top right of your screen.

The automated troubleshooters are separated into categories such as *Programs* and *Hardware and Sound* to make it easy to find what you are looking for. Each troubleshooter takes you through a series of questions to help it diagnose and repair problems.

Summary

In this book, I've guided you through everything you need to get started with Windows 8. You can use your computer to have fun, share things with friends and family, or work and be productive. I hope you've found it helpful.

I offer additional help and support, including tutorial videos, all of which you can see at my website *http://www.thelongclimb.com*. If I were to finish this book with one simple piece of advice, it is this: you shouldn't panic when something

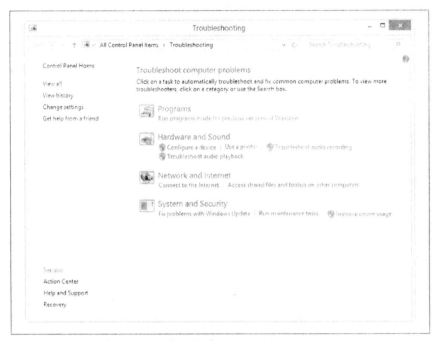

Figure 12-8. Using the automated troubleshooters

goes wrong. Your computer still isn't as dependable as your microwave and can stop working or misbehave occasionally. Don't get duped into spending money on expensive technical support.

I would suggest visiting my website for more help and working through the fixes and repairs to Windows 8 that I have detailed in this book.

Whatever you do with your computer, though, I sincerely hope you enjoy using Windows 8.

About the Author

Mike Halsey is the author of several Windows books, including *Troubleshoot and Optimize Windows 8 Inside Out*, *Beginning Windows 8*, and *Troubleshooting Windows 7 Inside Out*. He is a Microsoft MVP (Most Valuable Professional) awardee and a recognized Windows expert.

He regularly makes help, how-to, and troubleshooting videos and holds live webcasts for O'Reilly on the first Thursday of every month. Other previous roles include several years as a club-singer and working as a photographer.

Mike lives in an eco-home in Sheffield (Yorkshire, UK) with his rescue border collie, Jed.

CPSIA information can be obtained at www.ICGtesting.com
Printed in the USA
LVOW120918021212

309743LV00002B/262/P